"This is a deeply authei
within the collective vulnerabi
honor it is to be a part of this timely work, a labor of love if ever
there was one. Each of our narratives is unique and yet deeply
connected by strong thematic fibers that include a quest to be
all that we truly are in a landscape that asks us to relinquish our
authentic selves as the entrance fee into the struggle to succeed.
Although each of the authors has accomplished impressive levels
of success, these are stories of the cost, the toll, and the eventual
triumph of our very souls. This is a collective declaration of a
commitment to succeed on our own terms and reclaim the beauty
and power of our deepest selves and the ancestors who sowed
their love and strength into us with their blood, sweat and tears.
We honor them in this book. We honor us in this book."

Linda Lausell Bryant, MSW, Ph.D
Latinx in Social Work Madrina

"Owning your own narrative is the true embodiment
of freedom. This book highlights wonderful narratives that
demonstrate the diversity of our Latina diaspora. Thank you for
this important work."

Lisette Nieves
President, Fund for the City of New York

"This book offers a much-needed perspective of Latinx social workers' tireless efforts to advance equity and justice. These are personal stories of those working on the frontlines and are rich in emotion, philosophy, conflict, hope, and determination as they strive daily to make a difference in the quality of life of their communities. This book serves as an inspiration to future generations of Latinx social workers and the collective impact they look to make."

Ana L. Oliveira
President & CEO of The New York Women's Foundation

Latinx in
SOCIAL WORK

Stories that heal, inspire and connect communities

ERICA PRISCILLA SANDOVAL, LCSW- SIFI

LATINX IN SOCIAL WORK

This book is a compilation of stories from numerous people who have each contributed a chapter and is designed to provide inspiration to our readers.

It is sold with the understanding that the publisher and the individual authors are not engaged in the rendering of psychological, legal, accounting or other professional advice. The content and views in each chapter are the sole expression and opinion of its author and not necessarily the views of Fig Factor Media, LLC.

For more information visit:
Latinx in Social Work, Inc. | www.latinxinsocialwork.com

Cover Design by DG Marco Álvarez & Layout by LDG Manuel Serna
Fig Factor Media, LLC | www.figfactormedia.com

Printed in the United States of America

ISBN: 978-1-952779-76-3
Library of Congress Number: 2021919528

In loving memory of my grandparents
Abuelita Laura (1926- 2015) y
Abuelito Luis (1923- 1974)

To the present and future social
workers, you are Essential, own your
greatness. This book is for you.

TABLE OF CONTENTS

ACKNOWLDEGEMENTS

This book was guided by God, as I prayed every day to help me find my purpose, and I finally did. To my spiritual nourishment and magical power of my Ancestors, thank you for creating a path and breaking down barriers for me to step into my greatness.

The authors who collaborated in Latinx in Social Work, without you, this book would not be possible. Jaqueline Camacho- Ruiz, you are my shining light and guide. Thank you for sharing space, believing in me, this project and all of us. Gabriela Hernandez Franch, Author Concierge, you are the backbone of this project and I loved collaborating with you.

My dear parents, you both drive me crazy; I cannot imagine my life any other way and would not change one thing. Your passionate love created me, and this book is a result of your LOVE.

Isabella, my favorite person in the whole world. I created this to help you navigate this beautiful cruel world, YOU are my biggest inspiration. You make me a better human.

Nick, the love of my life, for your emotional support and ensuring I remember to care for myself, I am eternally grateful.

My sisters, Jenn and Jackie, and my cousin, Nathalie, thank you for cheering me on and honoring my vision.

There are countless people that supported and funded this project. To Ana Oliveira, The New York Women's Foundation, Dr. Lisette Nieves and the Fund for the City of NY, thank you. This would not be possible without your generosity and financial investment.

To my Madrina, Dr. Linda Lausell Bryant (Social Work Godmother), I am in awe of your wisdom, generosity, and love. You continue to teach and guide me, and I am honored that you have passed the baton to me, because as you say, "the race must continue." Thank you for nurturing and supporting me and this book.

Kerry Watterson, my mentor from AFP NYC. You are an incredible fundraiser and human. You helped me give birth to this project and give it life. I am proud to be your mentee and now lifelong friend.

My heartfelt thanks to all the incredible mentors, teachers, supervisors, supporters in my social work career, especially Mavis Seehaus, LCSW, Pam Mastrota, Paul Deasy, LCSW-R, Richeleen, A. Dashield, MBA, Linda Joannidis, LCSW-R, Joanne Ponifielo, Charmaine Peart-HoSang, LMSW, Maria Girone, MSW, Dr. Edith Chapparo, PHD, LCSW-R, Ben Sher, LMSW and NYU Silver School of Social Work.

My friendships mean everything to me. Luisa Lopez, I am in awe of your brilliance. To support our social work community as two Latinx Leaders during the pandemic has been nothing short of extraordinary. Palante! Vanessa Alamo, my best friend for life. YOU are my number one supporter and have pushed me to be proud, strong and to own my greatness.

A huge shout out to all our marketing partners, and Fig Factor Media team Christine Borges, Lisa Welz, our editors, Juan Pablo Ruiz (creative director and website), Manuel Serna (designer), Anna Fischer (proofreader) and VA, Laura Alonzo. It takes a village.

INTRODUCTION

Latinx in Social Work is a book is about space: the space we take up, the spaces we create and nurture, and the spaces that have yet to exist, but are so crucial to the growth and development of Latinx social workers, mental health practitioners, executives, and professionals in all industries in this country—and beyond. This book is a revolutionary step in creating a movement that is committed to owning our own narratives, naming common but unspoken struggles and challenges, and driving our own healing from the past, while highlighting our successes and creating a space for hope for the future.

The impediments to Latinx success, both personal and professional, are myriad; we know the familiar litany of barriers that our people face. These barriers include costs (monetary and opportunity costs), insufficient academic preparation or access to information regarding higher education, and the generalized discrimination that people of color continue to endure. The cost is often of our dignity, and at times, our worth, as we are often challenged by oppressive systems that hurt our souls but thicken our skins.

Stepping into our greatness with the full richness of our cultures and heritage in spaces not designed or meant for us is a truly courageous decision. It is a decision often taken at great personal and professional risk, and one which can cause unease about our security and our future.

Advocating for yourself or your clients, requesting that raise, positioning yourself as a leader for a promotion, embarking on a new business, starting a family—these can all seem like harrowing challenges with unknown results. Often, we believe we are unprepared to undertake them; doubt of our abilities, and anxiety about overstepping our bounds prevent us from taking the plunge. We color within the lines and sometimes never turn the page. We feel each professional trauma compounded by that of our ancestors—and beyond.

I write to you today from a place of bottomless understanding, because I have felt all of these things and am continuously overcoming them. It does not get easier, and it still hurts, except now I am more equipped and know that I am not alone. I share space and community with all of you as we navigate our careers, mental health, and wellness.

Our wellbeing, our *bienestar,* has been at risk, and will continue to be if we are not aware of the harm, the harm caused by systems, by our own internalized voice, which often mirrors what we have been told, or worse, by not being in our greatness. Radical self-care is learning to advocate for yourself, believing you are ENOUGH, and celebrating your accomplishments. We do not often do this for ourselves, and continue to push harder and harder because we think we are not doing enough. But as has been the case for generations, we are doing more with less, with little acknowledgement or recognition of our accomplishments and contributions.

I think of our ancestors that did not have time to rest, to

heal, nor have the benefit of understanding the harm done to them. For them we must rest, heal, reflect, and honor their labor by understanding the intergenerational experience and transformation. We are them, and they are us. We will not be silenced, and we will bring light and grace with love in celebration of our wins and our greatness. This is what our authors do: own their greatness.

My utmost desire is that by implementing some or all the skills and strategies demonstrated by the phenomenal people included in this book, you will find that your life, both personal and professional, will change in a fundamentally positive way. The goal of my work, and my life, is to provide you with the tools to understand and manifest the power of YOU in ALL spaces, so that this movement can continue for ourselves and our communities. This movement will foster deeper, more authentic conversations, healing and beneficial relationships, with ourselves, with each other, and with society as a whole.

I was taught to never give up. 'Keep your head up,' 'si se puede,' 'palante'—and so I kept going and did not turn back, despite feeling depleted and fatigued. While having chronic life stressors—such as the economic crisis, the pandemic, Mr. George Floyd's death leading to a year of protests, upheaval, and a divided country—I picked myself up almost immediately, and began to imagine a place where all our voices would be heard, where we could elevate each other.

These have been challenging times for our communities and for our country—and for us. To help me heal the wounds exposed by the pandemic, I have emerged myself in my servant leadership, as a volunteer leader for Prospanica NY, Latino Social Work Coalition, and National Association of Social Workers NYC. Collaborating with like minded individuals and supporting our communities has been a salve to the feelings of discomfort and sorrow that the pandemic has brought to the forefront, though it was not enough.

I recall that as a mentor with Prospanica NY, I received a thank you gift from Dr. Damary Bonilla-Rodriguez (I call her *doctora*); the gift she gave me was the book *Today's Inspired Latina*, an anthology series of inspirational Latina stories. I read each story, and they touched places in my soul. I envisioned creating that space for social workers, and so I embarked on the journey of creating this book.

As I met with each author, I realized the many commonalities and the beauty of our differences. Each of these authors has a unique and deep history and each is ready to unpack and name the harm of oppressive practices. In these pages you will see what it looks like in the trenches, where these often-unseen warriors create real, tangible, and positive impact in their communities.

These incredible social workers have poured their heart out and owned their narratives. You will see how unique each of these leaders is, and how our collective voice has become louder, prouder, and stronger. What we all share is a desire that our narratives give you hope and inspire you to own, create, and nurture spaces for yourself, for others, and for many more of US. Together, we rise.

This is unrelated to my position with NASW-NYC; I am not acting in my capacity as an officer of NASW-NYC.

Erica Priscilla Sandoval, LCSW-SIFI

PREFACE

Social workers are everywhere. They're in community-based organizations, in government agencies, in hospitals, in private practice, and in schools (though not nearly enough). Social workers are professionals whose unique skills and training are beneficial to every work environment. But as ubiquitous as social workers are, Latinx social workers are fewer in number.

Although the field is beginning to change, social work has historically been expensive to study and become licensed in, hostile toward practitioners of color, and dismissive of calls for communities to be served by social workers with similar lived experiences. Thanks to the Latino Social Work Coalition and Scholarship Fund, Inc., the number of Latinx social workers has been growing in recent years. However, their numbers lag behind the rate of the Latinx population in the United States, which grew 23% from 2010–2020, so that Latinx people now make up 19% of the country.

With Latinx social workers accounting for only 11.3% of all social workers nationwide, the profession remains ill-equipped to meet the needs of a population that increasingly speaks Spanish, lives in mixed immigration status households, and navigates political, economic, and social systems that further marginalize these communities. A social worker who speaks the local community's language, understands their cultural references, and is personally familiar with the systemic challenges the community faces can be the difference between a client being receptive and open to help and a client feeling alienated by the person or professional who is ostensibly there to support them. Despite this, the system as it exists today treats Latinx social workers and clients as an afterthought.

The goal of this book is to ensure that those experiences do not remain unexamined and unspoken. Rooted in her identities as a Latina, immigrant, first-generation social worker, and President of the New York City chapter of the National Association of Social Workers, Erica Sandoval creates a space for Latinx social workers to share their stories, their struggles, and their successes. In the pages ahead, she is amplifying the narratives about the successes and challenges faced by Latinx social workers, executive leaders, and changemakers, told in their own words. Each chapter will make other social workers and agents of change feel represented in a profession that can do more to elevate and appreciate these experiences.

Introduced into social work curricula, this book highlights leaders who understand the value of cultural humility and competence first-hand. It shines a light on the severe impact that the shortage of Latinx social workers has on our communities and will impress upon students—and their schools of social work— the urgent need for well-trained professionals to support an ever-increasing and vulnerable population that values their help.

In a testament to Erica Sandoval's commitment to the bright future of Latinx social workers, part of the book's proceeds will be donated to the Latino Social Work Coalition and Scholarship

Fund, Inc., an organization that has proved vital to supporting a pipeline of culturally competent social workers committed to their communities.

Latinx communities continue to face staggering rates of COVID cases, hospitalizations, and deaths, as well as job loss and increasing poverty. These challenges crystallize the need for communities of color to be served by social workers who share their cultural, linguistic, and community ties.

Hopefully, this book will change that. It will elevate Latinx social workers in the profession. Social work schools should incorporate this book into the curriculum. It can provide a mirror to Latinx students who will see themselves and the diversity of their experiences reflected in the profession. It elevates Latinx social workers to a level of scholarship normally reserved for Black and White social workers. In these pages are tales of people finding their passion, seeing the value of cultural humility and linguistic competence first-hand, and experiencing the impact of the shortage of Latinx social workers.

Gale A. Brewer
Manhattan Borough President

MADRINA

In this book we name and identify social work leaders as a *"madrina"* known as "God mothers", a woman who acts as a mentor, sponsor, patroness, or supporter to our growth, career and our profession. They lead the way, open and create space, pass the baton and help us grow and elevate.

"I'm honored to be considered a *'Madrina'* or Godmother to this project and to Erica Sandoval, the amazing woman who has birthed it. Being a *madrina* means that while I am still striving, growing and developing, I am also sowing what I have learned from my journey thus far into the next generations because our struggle for progress as a people will continue beyond my lifetime. The baton must be passed and the race must continue. Being a *madrina* means that I have a responsibility to nurture and support your development, to share what I have learned, and to play the roles that my journey has equipped me for, in service of our collective progress."

Dr. Linda Lausell Bryant
Clinical Associate Professor
NYU Silver School of Social Work

AUTHOR CHAPTERS

A THOUSAND LITTLE CUTS

ERICA PRISCILLA SANDOVAL, LCSW-SIFI

HOLY GUACAMOLE

"Wow, you speak English so well! You don't even have an accent! When did you come from Mexico?" a White customer asked. I remember the uneasy rush of blood to my face and pain in my stomach, as I composed myself to gather my thoughts and respond. I didn't reply with anger, I just said I am from Ecuador and came to this country when I was four, with a smile. I didn't realize then how harmed I was. I was working as a waitress at Rosa Mexicano, Lincoln Center in New York City and in college full-time, while raising my daughter as a single mother.

Of course, I knew consciously that my reaction would impact my tip, and that gratuity paid my bills and fed my daughter. It is so daunting to realize that our livelihood can be impacted by one reaction, one response, one decision, and so many times I remained silent at places of work for fear of losing income. This caught up to me.

In a conversation I had this year with one of my brilliant colleagues, Amelia Ortega, we were unpacking how painful it feels to enter trusted places and then be harmed. This predominantly happens in schools, classrooms, professional groups, and jobs, where we tend to spend most of our time. We can experience institutional betrayal, feel undermined, erased, not validated, not seen, not heard, and constantly triggered.

EMOTIONAL DEBT

In 2020, I began to feel more intensely, and processed deeply after being laid off for the first time in my life. I was in a senior level position at a nonprofit, barely there a year when the world turned upside down. It was not a surprise, since people of color are often faced with disproportionate job loss, underpaid, and experience hiring bias. We were also experiencing a pandemic, and job insecurity was at an all-time high.

I began to explore some patterns, and realized the pain I was feeling was stemming from not being heard and seen. It was not due to being laid off, it was due to the harm caused while I was employed. I felt undermined and extremely harmed by two colleagues that left me out of meetings, off emails, and would exclude me from important decisions related to my team and department. One was a direct report and another a director.

The common theme was they were White, and their voices louder than mine. This harmed my wellbeing. I began to lose sleep, eat more, and feel depressed. I would work harder, and never felt like it mattered. I felt betrayed. I felt discounted and not valued for my contributions, social work skills, and experience.

As a person of color, this toxic behavior caused great harm. I began to question, *am I good enough? Do I not deserve to be here? Was I smart enough?* It caused me a lot of pain. I obsessively started to pay off all my debt, barely spent any money, and began to study for my clinical exam again, while waiting for my last day to come. I went into financial distress mode. My family has always carried a great deal of financial distress and trauma, and this triggered what started long ago.

MIS ABUELOS

My *abuelita* (grandmother) Laura was married at the age of fifteen, and would rather have played basketball than become someone's wife. She married an amazing man, my abuelito (grandfather) Luis, and they had six children together. She came from a family of entrepreneurs; they had farms, stock, land, and that developed into businesses. She was a hardworking woman, and they were very respected and admired for the wealth they built together.

My *abuelito* would help many families by co-signing on loans and helping people get settled. This began to impact the family, since many people were not paying their debt. Their generosity was seen as admirable, but it was also their downfall. People do not always keep their word, and this caused a great deal of harm, as they slowly began to lose their wealth. This financial distress impacted generations.

Many unforeseen circumstances led to my abuelita's migration to the United States. My abuelito died in a traumatic car accident when I was one-year-old. I was in the car with my abuelitos and another family member, Maria. He managed to save my life, and my abuelita helped me out and carried me to safety. It was the worst day of my family's life.

My *abuelita* became a young widow with six children and a grandchild. She had severe PTSD, and was grieving an incredible loss while processing a traumatic experience on her own. I believe my abuelita's decision making after that was clouded due to the multiple traumas she was experiencing and were unrepaired. She became overwhelmed and an easy target. People stole from her, discounted her, and financially abused her. She continued to lose money due to ill decisions she made, and her business was impacted. She was a successful entrepreneur, as a restaurant owner, but was not able to maintain her wealth. Her business and wealth were taken from her, but she never lost her grit.

I was young when this happened in Quito, Ecuador. I didn't know her business was no longer her own. I remember vividly walking among schoolgirls with perfectly pressed uniforms one day. I was four years old when I got up from a very comfortable stoop of my paternal grandparents' tailor shop, and asked the schoolgirls to help me find my way to a familiar destination, my abuelita's restaurant. She had recently migrated to Miami, and I did not know where she was. Her restaurant was a few blocks away. I crossed streets and hectic avenues with help from each schoolgirl as they kept passing me on to the next group that was heading in the same direction.

I didn't know how to get there, but I knew where I was going. I was not lost; in fact, I was guiding them to my destination. They helped me arrive safely and I hoped to see my abuelita, but instead I was surrounded by other family members. They recognized me and called my mother. Everyone was hysterical. My father was in shock and panic, and had to immerse his head in a well filled with cold water. My mother, screaming and crying, found her way to me. I was lost for thirty minutes.

TRANSLATOR, PLEASE!

My parents were struggling in their marriage. They were barely twenty years old and navigating being teen parents. My mother worked long hours in a travel agency, and hustled daily to ensure my grandmother made it to the U.S. safely. She brought my abuelita's airline ticket and had to pay back the debt while ensuring we had everything we needed. I was confused, sad, and lonely.

My parents were having volatile fights. I remember being potty trained and neither of them would help me up. They would just keep fighting. Later in life, I asked my mom, "What were you and dad always fighting about?" Her response was not surprising—money and trust. My mother and I left Ecuador a couple of months after my abuelita, and the trauma continued.

This beautiful country had so much to offer. I remember how delicious the food tasted and how beautiful the clothing was. My mother made sure I was always well dressed and never hungry. Though we lived in poverty and were displaced for a few months, I always felt safe. I was with my abuelita again, and that was all that mattered.

Intergenerational trauma has been a prominent theme in our family. It has been handed over to us, just as some families hand over generational wealth. Our poverty was due to migrating to this country unequipped and traumatized. In the years that followed, we were faced with adversity, yet the grit my mother and grandmother had was undeniably stronger.

I remember having to learn English and translate for my abuelita and my parents. After my parents reunited, I lived with my parents, my abuelita, and two uncles, Tio Jaime and Tio Rene, who recently migrated to the U.S. None of us spoke English, and this was a struggle, but we managed.

I felt embarrassed when people made negative comments. Their employers would exploit them, and at times I would have to translate and advocate on their behalf. It was exhausting.

I acted out in school and "misbehaved" during my younger years, probably due to all the stress in my childhood. I needed a social worker; we all could have used one to support our migration and multiple traumas, though I do not think there were any in my neighborhood that spoke Spanish, and we lacked access to services.

PURA VIDA!

My parents had a dream: to return to their native country, Ecuador, as most immigrants do. They worked hard, bought land, and built their homes. There was always this unsettling feeling in the air, as if the wind carried a secret, saying, *we don't belong here.*

They went back to their beautiful country. I say that in a loving voice, because that country was not mine. The United States became my country, and my identity was embedded in Astoria Park, Queens, New York. The hot dogs and Italian ice cream after the pool, was *pura vida*. I'd rather starve than move to Ecuador.

So, they left with both my sisters, and I stayed with my *abuelita*. I was nineteen years old. I barely could feed myself, pay the rent, and commute to school. I managed though; I hustled, I worked hard. I had my abuelita down the block, roommates, and barely any savings. It was the best and worst time of my life. I was not able to focus or concentrate in school, and so I dropped out.

I was married, divorced, and ready to focus on my studies. It took being a divorced single mother with limited resources. I was the first in my family to graduate from college. I attended BMCC and then Baruch, and graduated with a degree in adolescent development.

The economy crashed and my parents returned—and had to start all over. My mom applied at hospital. Again, she asked me to translate, and when I spoke to HR, it hurt to share she did not get the job due to her limited English. The woman then asked if I was interested in applying for a position in the social work department. They needed a bilingual, Spanish speaking associate at the Hospital for Special Surgery.

Doing the thing I hated most, translating, launched my career in social work. After working there for four years, I applied and was accepted to NYU Silver School of Social Work. I spent countless hours in the NYU library and my office at HSS. I hardly spent time with my daughter, Isabella.

In 2011, I was the first to graduate with my master's in social work. It was the proudest moment of my entire life. I never thought I could accomplish this incredible feat. My parents provided me with what they could, but I had to fend for myself while raising Isabella. I had so many barriers, but I also had courage, passion, and perseverance. I realized I inherited grit. I never stopped, never looked back, stayed consistent, and kept my eye on the prize.

My social work career has been incredible yet challenging. In every position, I would bring a lens of cultural humility and challenge inequity. I was a strong advocate for families that could not speak English and were marginalized by oppressive practices. I had to challenge individuals in higher positions of power and call them into understanding their unconscious bias. I would name systemic racism in practices, policies, and procedures, to help create change to support equity and inclusion. When I obtained my LCSW, I became a business owner and entrepreneur, and started my private practice. My practice filled in less than three weeks, as there is a shortage of Latinx social workers needed to serve the Latinx community.

I am one of three social workers in my family. My two younger sisters, Jennifer and Jackie, graduated from Columbia School of Social Work and New York University Silver School of Social Work, respectively. Between the three of us, we can move mountains.

We were raised to honor and love our parents. The three of us have our different reasons on why we chose this profession, yet I believe the one common theme is to *make our parents proud.* Our mother, Laura Piedad and father, Rodrigo, worked hard and built a legacy. Our beloved grandmother died in 2015, surrounded by her family. Most of us are college graduates. We are here on the sweat and hours of their labor, and hope our work and education will bring generational wealth and reduce intergenerational trauma.

REFLECTION

Navigating your career is not easy when compounded with multiple life stressors. When working with your clients, understand that they come in with histories, long before they were born. The thread of their makeup goes back generations. See them, hear them and support them with a culturally humble lens. If you are becoming a social worker, do your own work, so you can be caring for yourself as you will be caring for many of us. Stay consistent, focus on the prize, and find your grit.

- What is a microaggression?
- How can I show up for others, while showing up for myself?

ABOUT THE AUTHOR

Erica Priscilla Sandoval, LCSW-SIFI is Founder of Sandoval CoLab, a psychotherapy and consulting group. As a passionate, licensed clinical therapist and consultant, she is dedicated to promoting diversity, equity, and inclusion (DEI). She is committed to amplifying the voices and businesses of incredible Latinx social work leaders and social justice-focused changemakers, who are healing and inspiring communities.

She partners with organizations, universities, nonprofits, health care facilities, medical, and corporate professionals to provide access to resources to advance teams and help employees and students thrive. Most recently, she co-founded Employee Network Allyance, a space for allyship for today and tomorrow's employee network leaders who help each other succeed.

Erica holds a post master's degree in clinical adolescent psychology and a master's in social work from New York University, Silver School of Social Work. She currently serves as a volunteer leader as president of the board of directors for National Association of Social Workers NYC, the largest organization for professional social workers worldwide.

Her work focuses on the intersectionality of behavioral health, social disparities, trauma, and human development. She serves as advisor for Latino Social Work Coalition and Prospanica NY. Her successful career earned her numerous awards. She is regularly invited to be a guest speaker, moderator, and panelist by well-known organizations. Her greatest pride is raising her twenty-one-year-old daughter, Isabella, as a single mother, who she considers her biggest teacher. As a proud immigrant from Ecuador, her passion is fueled by supporting the community she is a part of.

Erica Priscilla Sandoval, LCSW-SIFI
President and Founder of Latinx in Social Work Inc.
Erica@latinxinsocialwork.com
http://www.latinxinsocialwork.com/

Madrina

MY JOURNEY TO SOLIDARITY AS A BLACK AND JEWISH LATINA

DR. LAURA QUIROS, PH.D., LMSW

"We are restorers of the soul, we are healers, grounded in a mission of social justice."

My themes for this chapter are intergenerational trauma, legacy, and solidarity. Adhering to the social work person-in-environment framework, I wanted to start where my story began and end where I am today, all with the understanding that the profession of social work is a journey—and a transformational one, if you are open to it.

It is also an identity. One of the most precious things about social work is that, if you lean into it, self-evolution is not only possible but necessary, because social work is a profession that works with the human condition. It is a relational profession that requires the use of self. Who we are in our many identities always show up in the room, and so the question becomes: how do you use yourself to form connections and help individuals, groups, and communities overcome obstacles?

This crucial and intentional use of self is not taught or honored in traditional social work. I have always been perplexed by the traditional clinical teachings of non-disclosure. My students come to me having learned somewhere along their educational social work journey, that disclosure is "bad" and disruptive to the therapeutic alliance. They adhere so strictly to the formal practice interventions that they are unable to locate themselves and then use their unique selves and subsequent vulnerability to share stories that may in fact, deepen the human connections between themselves and their clients. The odds of clients engaging in a transformational experience are much greater when we model courage, lean into vulnerability, and allow ourselves to be seen, and one way we can do this is by storytelling.

Ultimately, the person, group, and community experiences healing through the relationship, and so why would we as a profession shy away from sharing ourselves and our stories? I understand that with sharing of self, there has to be an intentionality, mindfulness, and purpose, but once we do that self-work, the possibilities are endless because who we are and the stories we choose to share cannot be disconnected from the work. Part of social work training must involve this self-work I just mentioned.

We ask clients to share the deepest and rawest parts of themselves, yet are we open and brave enough to do the same?

Self-work involves the uncovering of who we are and how we show up in the room. It involves sitting in therapy and other quiet moments of accountability around our own traumas and around the ways we have been socialized. Crucial to this work is the intentional use of self in order to open up the spaces for others. It is a modeling of sharing in boundaried ways that allow for truth telling, connection, community building, and healing

Let me locate myself for you: I identify as a Black cis-gendered Latina who is also Jewish. I am a single mom of two girls, Isabel, seven, and Carla, thirteen. I am a professor, consultant, friend, sister, mentor, and partner. All of these identities show up in the classroom and in my personal and professional relationships. I grew up in a home with a white, Jewish mother and a Black, Latino father.

I have written that line so many times in my publications and drafts for my talks, yet each and every time, I am faced with a new image of what that looks like for me as an adult—and what that looked like for me as a child. I make this distinction between our childhood and our adult selves early on in this chapter, because so much of my personal work has been to live in the present.

To understand the emotional and psychological energies I was, and sometimes still am holding onto, and why, and finally to understand how to self soothe that young child, so that she could show up in all her glory as an adult. For me, as a social work educator, I have a responsibility to understand myself and my story on a deep level in order to show up sincerely for my students, for my clients, and for my children.

INTERGENERATIONAL TRAUMA

As a child, my life looked and felt like a home that was split in two. On one side, I had my mom's very New York and Jewish family; great grandparents, Rubin and Dora who lived in Co-Op city, Rubin was a tailor who fought hard for Union rights, sewed my dolls' clothes and Bubby, as we called her, made the most delicious egg creams and sat for hours telling me stories of my heritage. I had a grandfather whom I called "Papa," he was a jeweler, and then there was my matriarchal grandmother who I called "Nana" and who provided much of my childcare growing up.

I sat through long Passover Seders with my cousins in Long Island, the same cousins who owned a prestigious Summer Day Camp. I remember the traditions, the values of education, a purposeful driven life, and that my Jewish world was, looked, and felt, very white.

My father and I were the darkest members of the family, and that did not go unnoticed. I remember the time I went to Florida to visit my grandparents and was told I was "too dark" to swim in the pool. My Papa loved me and also did not believe in interracial marriages. While the Jewish members of my family understood what hate felt like and had experienced their own intergenerational trauma because of their Jewish identity, they were racist and lived in their protected identity of whiteness.

It was when I was with my father and his family that I felt more of a sense of belonging. The resemblance between me and my aunts and cousins were obvious: our complexion and curly hair, the food, music, loud and passionate ways of being felt familiar, yet on some level I always remained an outsider for a few reasons.

For starters, my father made the decision early on not to teach my brother and I Spanish. Spanish was his first language, yet because of years of discrimination and the repeated demands of *"English only,"* he felt very strongly that he did not want to inflict the same suffering on my brother and I. Language is always a strong marker of identity, and when you do not speak the language of your culture, there is a felt exclusion, a de-legitimizing that takes place both externally and internally. Second, the intergenerational trauma that my father experienced because of his race and culture found its way in our home, and while I spent some summers in Puerto Rico, I was not as immersed in the culture as some of my cousins were. Lastly, my mother was white and Jewish, and so for many years I did not feel like I had the right to claim a Black and Latina identity, because it felt like an act of treason. As a result, much of my childhood and early adulthood was spent figuring out who I was and how to claim all the parts of myself.

LEGACY

My mom passed away the summer of 2021, just as the world started to open back up after a year and a half of living under the COVID-19 pandemic. She survived the pandemic; had gotten her vaccine and we had fallen back into our weekly routine of her visiting with my girls. Since her passing, I have been thinking a lot about legacy. The power and glory of my mom lived in her ability to love unconditionally, to be in relationship, and to find the beauty and good in everyone. She celebrated the lives of those in her circle—cakes and candles at every birthday, always wanting the closeness of family around her. She lived up to the stereotype of the Jewish mother—sacrificing, devoted, and ever-present.

My children leaned into these qualities as did my brother, and I would imagine her closest friends, and co-workers. As for my girls, my mom knew their special meals, just the right books for each of them, and how to love them for what they each needed, which was often very different. Izzy benefited from lots of cuddles and the tickle monster, and Carla from long talks about pre-teenage angst, the challenges of her parents' divorce, and special Netflix shows they watched—my mom always made sure to watch the same shows Carla was, and then they would sit, play cards, and talk about the details. She parented my girls in the most loving, compassionate, and non-judgmental ways from the day they arrived.

While my girls leaned into this power and glory, for me it always felt more complicated, and much of that complication came from our different racial identities and the ways in which the world responded to us and how we navigated the world. I have spent a ton on time contemplating why that was. At times, I felt like I needed something different. It was not that I didn't want to crawl into her arms every time I saw her; I believe now it was because I was processing how to embrace her approach to life and her identity as a white and Jewish woman, with my own need to lean into my own Black and Latina identity—and my own power.

Even into my early fourties, I was still figuring out what that was. And after much personal work in therapy and with close friends, I now understand that my mom and I were very different women but women who nonetheless learned how to see each other for who we were. People talk about how complicated relationships can be between mothers and daughters. And only now do I fully realize why—my mom helped me understand that I needed to do the hard work to see my own power and own my identity as a Black Latina who is also Jewish. She helped me understand how loving people unconditionally is complicated and can be messy, but it is crucial. I now realize as a fully grown woman myself, the gifts she gave me to be able to figure out these things for myself, in addition to loving others around me so deeply. And she has left me with one final gift.

There is something in me that has shifted since that Wednesday, June 16, 2021 at 2 a.m. when she passed away; it is a shift of responsibility, of thinking deeply and intentionally about my legacy, about what I inherited, and what my mom has given to all of us. Her deep love, my connection to Judaism, the many layers of being a mother. And with that, I am striving to embody her power and glory of love, generosity of spirit, and patience. I can see now clearly the gifts she left behind.

Who am I and what have I inherited? I learned to ask these questions during my time working as a facilitator for an arts and cultural organization called Reboot. I had the privilege of facilitating six session sessions on the intersections of Judaism and Anti-Black Racism. It was during these sessions that I began to understand what solidarity meant, and how my multicultural and biracial identity was in fact an embodiment of that solidarity.

SOLIDARITY

As I shared, growing up, the solidarity around a shared identity of the intergenerational trauma of racism and anti-Semitism did not exist. As an adult, I often imagine what my childhood would have been like if I was taught the shared identity in groups of people who have experienced hate, who were both discriminated against because of being different from the white and Christian hegemony. Instead, there was a fractioning of my identities. Although I spent many years in therapy, I never had a therapist, or social worker, who helped me see my identity as an act of solidarity.

I cannot separate my Blackness from my Latinness— and nor do I want to. My passion, the way I express myself, my emotionality, and love of Latin food and music adds to my Black and Latina identity. I also lean into my Jewish values of higher order, purpose, education, generosity, kindness and social justice. I am complete in all of this beautiful complexity. And so, as social workers, how do we help first ourselves, and then our clients, show up better for ourselves and then for one another? How do we find solidarity amongst the many colors of our culture? We are restorers of the soul and we are healers, grounded in a mission of social justice.

REFLECTION

Social work is important today because it is a profession of healers, and healing that offers us the opportunity to build sincere relationships with ourselves and with others. We are restorers of the soul. We are in unprecedented times, emerging from a pandemic and bearing witness to individual and collective trauma and disparity. I could not think of a better time for this profession, when there is a yearning for community building and healing, when there is a need to diversify spaces.

Let's build in inclusive practices and lean into equity. Social work connects the micro lived experiences with larger macro systems as a way for us to move closer to understanding the impact systems have on the human condition and move further away from individual deficits. It is a profession grounded in a person-environment framework, and we cannot separate the person from their environment. Ultimately, social work is a profession that calls for social justice work, that requires courage and a willingness to constantly self-examine ourselves and the systems we are a part of and participate in. Social work is an invitation to imagine and then create, a loving world.

Locate yourself: what brought you to this profession? How has that original purpose shifted? What do you feel challenged by? What are your acts of solidarity?

ABOUT THE AUTHOR

Laura Quiros, PhD., LMSW has been an associate professor of social work at Adelphi University for the past twelve years. She teaches social work practice at the doctoral and master's level. Her research and scholarly interests focus on the trauma informed care from a social justice lens. The common thread in her consulting, teaching, and scholarship is elevating complexity and furthering the mission of social justice, including diversity and inclusion.

She coaches, trains and facilitates dialogues with executive-level staff across higher education, corporate, and nonprofits to dig deep and sincerely connect to diversity and inclusion. Some of this work involves gently pushing the boundaries of overcoming the resistance to talking candidly about whiteness and unpacking diversity and inclusion work. Much of this has been accomplished through relationship building. She uses her relationship building and clinical skills as a way to foster connection, inclusion and empathic accountability. The intersection for her is clear, as a woman of color from a very multicultural background, she could only survive through relationship building. Negotiating her identity required her to create safe enough and brave spaces in order to survive and thrive. Her practice is one of liberation, love, and generosity.

THE RE-EDUCATION OF THE
BLACK LATINA

———

KAREN CIEGO, LCSW

REAL SOCIAL WORK ORIENTATION

Should I wrap this up or what? I absentmindedly twirled the mug and looked at it, not seeing it. The mug had been a gift from work, and it was the last thing to pack up from my cubicle before going into private practice. This place was where I got my first social work job and I hopscotched through different positions over the years.

Tracing back my steps to the beginning placed me amidst aspiring social workers at a MSW job fair. I'd come to check on a bilingual social worker position I had applied for online. I was counting down to finishing grad school, sick of writing papers. My stipend-paying second year internship had just wrapped up, and it was time to stop playing games.

When it was my turn, I stepped tenaciously towards the woman in charge of the job I just knew was mine. Ripping a page from the interview prep workshops I taught, I shook her hand firmly. I joked about my "lost" application and waited for her to laugh, to see me. Her slow elevator eyes took me in. I prayed that my bright white blouse was stain-free because of my habit of touching my face and smearing dark brown makeup on my tops. Finally, tilting her head and shaking it apologetically, "You have to speak Spanish," she stated.

I was invisible. "My first language is Spanish. I learned English in school, actually," I insisted with a wide smile. But it was too late. The force of the blow threw me back to a time before having my first daughter in college, before getting married and divorced, before getting married again and having another daughter, before going back to school, before finding my passion for helping my people. I stood, once again, not knowing where I belonged.

Afterward, I dragged a shell of myself through the tables making dumb small talk about this or that low-paying job. Having had a colorful string of jobs for ten years before returning to school, my expectations weren't high, but they weren't that low either. This is a master's degree, last I checked. According to my bank account I was about to be broke, though. I returned to the table where my job was not my job and applied for another position there. I heard they paid well, at least.

I then went home, undressed, and cried. Weeks later, my pride took a backseat because we all have to eat. I accepted an offer from none other than the infamous place. That decision was not without its hard lessons, though.

SWALLOWING MY PRIDE

Learning about white supremacy on paper is one thing; living it consciously is another. That was clear to me years later, when I sat in the closet-like office of my boss—thunderstruck. In the middle of my rehearsed argument for my staff to get a chance to grow professionally, she thought it important to casually inform me that some of the social workers I supervised weren't cut out for management positions. *Why even bother*, she went on. There weren't any opportunities anyway. I stared at her thin lips, defeated. She patted me on the head with her words and thanked me for trying. My Black and Brown team—myself included—had no choice but to be excellent just to get through the door.

The urge to fight set my soul ablaze. Somehow, I wasn't hauled away by security because... bills. I wished my work sister were there to check if my bottom lip quivered when I swore—I looked unflappable. She told me the lip always announced the truth of my anger.

But for times when there were no witnesses, I devised many self-soothing techniques. One of my tricks was stealing glances at an invisible camera on the wall, giving it the "you can't make this shit up" face. Another handy tool was to make believe that it was all a prank, and that the cameras and crew would suddenly storm in teasing me. I was only too ready to throw my head back relieved. *"Oh mah gah! Ya got me!"* I would say. And when I really hurt, I made mental notes of the microaggressions and invalidations for my one-woman debrief show. In it I would reenact the stingers and smart retorts I wished I had the bolas to spit in real life. Releasing the injuries from my body through laughter saved me and my job many, many times. It also made for good entertainment at the office.

DISCONNECTED AND RECONNECTED

But this last time wasn't funny. *Pero mira pues, Karen...* Mami said, warming up to reset my perspective by painting a picture of third-world country struggles, as usual. She'd go on about the lack of access to education, money, power, and privilege. Of course, I appreciated her point of view. I wasn't trying to dispute her truth. Making her way to this country was hard, and I owed her more than my life for ensuring I finished college while living under her roof with a baby many years earlier.

I had come to understand that she and I were talking about the same demons; mine were first-generation, but still the same. Words shook in my throat as I described the helplessness of occupying a front row seat to denial of access, and I worried that her world and mine were so different now that my suffering got lost in translation.

But now I was a whole, professional woman on my own with my daughters. Mami came through with Garifuna dinners from time to time; the sincerity of her offerings was enough to shrink the gulf between us. I rarely took food to work, preferring to throw my money away on overpriced Manhattan lunches. But there was this one time, though. The ladies at work simply had to taste Mami's *tapado*. I packed it up tight and brought it with me. Struck by inspiration, I converted my leftovers into the main course of an impromptu farewell for my work sister. She had decided to leave the job and unleash all her Black Woman Power. I was proud of her and sad to see her go, but more proud than sad. So, we moved quickly, hunting for bowls and Tupperware to accommodate anyone with an appetite. We were eager to eat, manifest, and talk shit.

This was my dry and bland place of work, so it felt odd yet familiar to be surrounded by a Black and Brown sisterhood that dipped spoons into warm, savory coconut milk broth and spit fish bones into napkins. We cackled and whispered in turns, sharing stories about love, ancestors, un-shattered ceilings, and our lives in our sacred space. The glow of the twinkling lights we kept on year-round gave our office the feeling of Christmas, and on this day in May, it felt right. We managed to carve out a nook for ourselves where we collectively knew that we were needed and not wanted. That was fine by us, because we belonged with each other.

WELL, I'LL BE...

"*Yes, I can,*" I said some years later. An uncle had taught me that was the only response to opportunities that came my way. I had just been tapped to complete Spanish language assessments and screen potential applicants at the upcoming MSW job fair. I knew good and well that it was convenient to my employer that I was worth double points in the diversity game for being Black and being Latina. Nonetheless, no one was more prepared for this than I was. Plus, my weary soul needed this win.

An added benefit was the chance to pick candidates who would make a good fit for my department. My plan was simple: I would hire who was needed, and pay special attention to those who possessed the values and qualities required to fulfill the needs of the people we served. What this meant was that the candidate would have to be authentic, humble, brilliant, and woke. I created this goal based on my direct work and as a supervisor of a diverse team of social workers.

In my mind, I casted each candidate as a supervisee and completed mini mock supervisions to understand if the mission lived in their hearts. This was my way of demolishing the farce of exceptionalism one hire at a time. It was my most fervent desire to shut up everyone who looked at me and thought, *now there goes a fine unicorn!*

I motioned the next person in line to head towards me. She stepped with confidence and talked me through her short but oh-so-perfect experience. Her understanding of the mission and the work was so strong that I marked her resume for her to be called in. Her skin looked like mine, and she did not speak a lick of Spanish. And she was everything we needed.

Over a year later, she sat with me and revisited our first encounter. She described how she'd been waiting nervously for her turn and with there being multiple representatives at my table, she was unsure whether to step forward when I motioned for her. She confessed that she had been afraid. I urged her to continue as she began to suck back her words. *"I heard you speaking Spanish to the people in front of me and, you know, I thought you wouldn't hire me because…"* I screwed up my face, not believing the words and dissolved into laughter. The irony.

GRACE AND PERSPECTIVE

It was funny to see the misconceptions about identity transcend time and place. Not too much later, I was on a bus ride heading home when I overheard three kids no older than fifteen who were clearly close friends. "You're not Black, you're Spanish," said one to a girl who looked Black to my eyes. And just like me, the girl stood quietly and accepted the assignment bestowed upon her by others who knew no better.

I wasn't sure why this was still amusing to me. In the second grade, my crush who looked like a member of Menudo told me with the same certainty that I was not Black but *trigueña.* I figured that if his cute Menudo self said that's what it was, that's what it was. Now, an entire lifetime later, it wasn't for me to intrude. Who was I to walk over to the kids' side of the bus and tell that girl who she was? Life and experience would task her with that responsibility of finding out.

Obviously dropping knowledge on kids who don't know me isn't my thing, but with my own girls, it's my priority to create a home for informed, conscious, nonjudgmental self-discovery. It seemed that life had gone out of its way to show me what it is to be Black, to be a Garifuna American, and to be Afro Latina, especially as a social worker working in White spaces. So, it's possible that our worlds will differ slightly, but it's a certainty in my mind that the demons that haunted Mami's generation and mine will evolve in my kids' lifetimes. I hope that my perspective also remains open to change, as not to create a chasm between us, because I have no idea how to make *tapado*. I have hope that we will be fine.

I swiveled in my chair, breathing through the memories, the mug dangling off my finger. I walked it over to the pantry, washed it, and dried it off. Then I set it gently in the waste basket.

REFLECTION

- What have you been taught about who you are *supposed* to be?
- What life lessons connected to your identity stick out the most? Are they negative/positive? Accurate/inaccurate?
- What can you do to extend grace to yourself as you navigate the world in your skin?

ABOUT KAREN CIEGO

Karen Ciego is a psychotherapist, clinical supervisor, public speaker, educator, and advocate for the healing of BiPoC. She has over eleven years of social work experience, many as a program coordinator in the healthcare system, wherein she contributed to several diversity initiatives. Karen led a high-achieving team of Black and Brown social workers towards clinical licensure—a personal goal near and dear to her heart. Under her supervision through the pandemic, her team implemented unparalleled culture-affirming interventions to serve populations most affected by COVID-19.

Karen is executive consultant of Clinicians of the Diaspora, LLC. and therapist to a roster of BiPoC professional women and mothers. Her therapeutic approach is informed by her lived experience as a first-generation Garifuna American raised in the South Bronx, where she lives with her brilliant and creative daughters. Karen provides clinical supervision, facilitates psychodynamic groups, teaches various social work courses, and takes naps occasionally. She inspires by way of humor, gratitude, and homegrown peace.

Karen Ciego
karenciego@gmail.com

LATINA, COURAGEOUS, STRONG, WOMAN: MY DESTINY

MADELINE MALDONADO, LCSW-R

Being the daughter of two immigrants from the Dominican Republic, growing up in "El Alto Manhattan" (Upper Manhattan) and then, at age twelve, moving to the Bronx, set the foundation for the love that I have for Latinos and the appreciation for our culture. Latinos are hard-working, resilient people with a great sense of humor and a love of life. I learned this from my parents growing up, and I saw it all around me in people who managed to smile, laugh, and dance, despite the most difficult life circumstances.

I was born in a working poor, immigrant community in New York City. By the mid 1980s, this community, like many others in New York, was in crisis from the drug epidemic and the subsequent crime and poverty that ensued. I was accustomed to seeing the empty crack vials on the school playground floor, and the men who spent their days drinking outside the bodegas and liquor stores in the community.

When I was eight years old, I told my father that I wanted to save the world. He smiled and told me that I could do that, that I could help make this world better. Little did he know that I really meant it, that I was speaking aloud what I now know is my purpose in this world: to help people and to make this world better.

Initially, I thought that my career would be in civil engineering or medicine. Interestingly enough, it was through working as a cashier at my father's supermarket while in high school and then as an administrative assistant at a medical practice in college, that I came to understand that I have a gift for connecting with people. To my surprise, at sixteen I had supermarket customers telling me about their personal lives in response to my asking, "How are you doing?" as I rung up their groceries.

At the medical practice, patients would share with me how they were anxious about getting a test result or were stressed because of their job; frequently they would share their personal lives with me. I was and still am deeply fascinated by people's experiences, their life stories, and their emotions and perspectives. I knew that while civil engineering and medicine were interesting and lucrative professions, I would never get to connect with people and truly impact their emotions and perspectives in those careers. At twenty-one, one of my college counselors told me about clinical social work, and it was like a lightbulb went off for me. I felt this overwhelming excitement that comes when you find a career that aligns with your life's purpose.

TRANSPARENT

While working at my two graduate school internships, I became aware that there was a tremendous shortage of Spanish-speaking clinical social workers. I was also deeply aware of how these clients were treated when they did not have a Spanish-speaking and Latino social worker as a provider and advocate. They were misdiagnosed, over-medicated, sometimes under-medicated, and their input didn't seem to matter in the decisions that were being made for their care. As I worked with these Black and Brown clients, I saw the faces of my own family members and recalled their own experiences navigating systems that did not seem to care about providing services to them. I made a decision while I was still in graduate school: I would be working in high need communities with African American and Latino clients.

My first job was as a mental health therapist in the South Bronx. This is the place where I learned to see beyond a client's illness or disabilities and to appreciate the community where I was working. The clients were so welcoming and never made me feel that I was inexperienced (although I was).

Next, I transitioned to macro social work, and moved on to community education. I spent my days going to schools, senior centers, hair salons, churches, and other organizations to promote mental health awareness and suicide prevention. This was before social media and the internet made sharing information possible with the click of a button. I had to hit the streets in the Bronx, network and engage in public speaking to get the message across. I really enjoyed getting to meet so many different people, and it was exciting to go to different neighborhoods every day.

I didn't enjoy having an open fire hydrant directed at me so that my dress would be drenched and become transparent (this was a prank the teenaged males liked to do to women on summer days). I felt like they could see through me—and they actually could. After this, I no longer wore dresses when I was working in the community. Despite the challenges, this job was the beginning of developing myself as a public speaker and learning to trust my voice as a social worker. It's a skill that I continue to use to this day as an adjunct professor and speaker on mental health panels and conferences.

I wish I could say that the micro-aggressions stopped as I continued with my career, or that they were less painful to experience. That feeling of shame about my Latina body dominated my choices in professional attire for many years. From slacks that were two sizes too big, to skirts that were loose and knee length, to layering cardigans over my clothing and saying it was due to me always being cold in the office; my closet was full of clothes that I felt I had to wear every day in order to be respected and taken seriously.

I still remember a colleague sharing aloud in the staff breakroom her perception of the reason for my high retention rate: "Your clients always show to sessions Madeline, it doesn't hurt that you're so beautiful." I was invisible or transparent again. With that one statement, my colleague "erased" twenty years of my professional experience and my knowledge of clinical interventions, and did so in front of our other colleagues.

However, it was different this time. I knew this was a form of microaggression called a microinsult, and I did not internalize her feelings and allow her to invalidate me. Instead, I immediately sought support from colleagues and friends that validated my experience and affirmed that I was not being too sensitive about her comment. I also meditated and prayed and affirmed my truth over and over: that my experience, skills, and my abilities are the reason I am successful with my clients. Becoming aware of what microaggressions are and how to overcome and cope with them is something I have taught my social work students and those I have supervised over the years.

I have become stronger from these experiences. My Latina body is not to be shamed. I no longer apologize for making you uncomfortable. I shed that professional wardrobe that didn't suit me because this does not make me less skilled. I love and appreciate my body for its curves and for its strength to not break under the violence of objectification, sexism, and microaggressions.

THE EMPTY CHAIR

When I was twenty-seven, I started thinking that it was time to start bringing my ideas as to how to run more effective mental health programs to life. I wanted to change how organizations

LATINX IN SOCIAL WORK

were being run in order to better serve African American and Latino clients. I decided that pursuing administrative roles would be the way to accomplish that, and I was hired as a clinical supervisor at a hospital.

This was my first experience supervising teams, and I began to figure out what kind of social work leader I wanted to become. I also learned that not everyone was happy that I was there. One of my colleagues, whom was a clinical supervisor in another department, made it very clear that she thought I was "too young" for the job. She also made it a point to never allow me to sit next to her at the weekly meetings. This is an example of ageism and systems that harm you. I remember crying in the bathroom several times because I could not understand why she did not like me. I learned a valuable lesson from working with her, though: you cannot make people like you, so you might as well do what you came to do and do it well. Once I stopped caring about or seeking her approval, I was able to thrive in that setting despite being harmed. I continued to focus, work hard, and to show the quality of my skills as a supervisor. I gained the attention of the clinic director, and when she moved on to another agency, she told me about an available position there.

At thirty, I became a clinic director; my dream came true! I was supervising a team of mental health therapists providing bilingual and bicultural outpatient mental health services, crisis intervention, and case management to Latino clients in the Bronx. Over the years, I have replicated my model for leading mental health clinics with teams of therapists and supervisors at several organizations. We had tremendous success working with African American and Latino men, women, and children. Some were even high-risk clients who were thought to be a danger to themselves or others.

There have been tremendous highs: such as being featured in the NASW's Hispanic Heritage Website as an "outstanding therapist" twice, becoming a Hunter College SEEK Department Hall of Fame Inductee, having several program audits cited as exemplary, and being invited to teach social work graduate school classes at Fordham University. There have also been challenges and lows, like working after the terrorist attacks on September 11, two of my therapy clients committing suicide within three months of one another, working until at least 2:00 a.m. many times during audits or while working on special projects, having to fire social workers for poor performance or unethical behavior, enduring the lingering stares and verbal harassment from a male boss and having to leave that job, and working during the COVID-19 pandemic.

I think of that empty chair next to me at the weekly meetings and how inadequate and insecure I felt when she moved away. I chose to sit there and I knew that I deserved to sit there. That empty chair motivated me to want to fill that space with social workers of color. And over the years, I have been able to sit at the head of the table and make room for all of us. For you….

MY SECRET SAUCE

I've learned that in social work, just like in life, you must grow and reinvent yourself in order to succeed to your highest potential. I opened up my social work consulting practice in 2015 and have dedicated this next phase of my career to evaluating children with developmental delays and disabilities. Most of the children I see are Latino or African American, many living in working poor communities like the one I grew up in. Most families are not familiar with mental health problems or developmental delays in toddlers and how to manage such conditions. Much of what I do is connecting with the families and seeking to understand what their concerns are. When there is a diagnosis (i.e. Autism Spectrum Disorder), I give it with dignity and compassion, and I try to provide information and hope that change is possible with treatment. I also advocate in my written reports for these children and families to be given the services that they need so that the child will be able to obtain their highest potential.

At the time that I am writing this, I will have been a social worker for twenty-one years. My legacy will be that I have helped to heal people and change their lives, thus causing a chain reaction within their own families. I am honored to have had thousands of clients over the years tell me their stories, share their hearts with me and in doing so, trust me with their lives.

I am resilient and brave. I have deep faith in God, and in my most difficult moments, I know that I can and will overcome. I always bet on me, and I have confidence in my gifts and abilities, even when I haven't figured out how things will come together. This is my secret sauce—and what sets me apart.

My resilience is my gift to my clients and other social workers; it's what I teach them, to fight for their emotional well-being, for their dreams, and to take a stand for what they want for themselves and their families. My hope for you reading my story is that you seek a career that fulfills your purpose, and that you choose to spread love and share your gifts with the world. I hope that you will see yourself as an agent of change for the most vulnerable people in our communities. But most of all, I hope that you remain authentic to who you are and where you come from—that's your secret sauce!

BEYOND

Social Work is so important today because we are the only career that combines social justice, social change, policy work and mental health. During 2020 and 2021, we have seen an increase in Americans with depression, anxiety, suicidality, post-traumatic stress disorder, and substance abuse. We have endured living in a pandemic, racial tensions, police brutality, riots, a surge in hate crimes, a rise in white supremacist groups, and a financial recession and record unemployment. Through it all, social workers on the front lines have marched for social justice, we have demanded social change, and we have continued to be there for our clients. Social Work is hard and requires courage and commitment. For each of us that succeeds, there is more work to be done—and more being brave. And I have absolutely no regrets.

REFLECTION

- What is the 'secret sauce' that sets me apart from other people?
- How have my experiences of microaggressions impacted what I see when I look in the mirror?
- What are ways I can overcome and cope with painful experiences and affirm my truth?
- How can I use my talents and skills to make a difference in the lives of other people?

ABOUT THE AUTHOR

Madeline Maldonado has over twenty years of experience in program administration, clinical supervision, professional trainings, and psychotherapy. She specializes in autism evaluations for children and adolescents. Madeline is the president and owner of Madeline Maldonado, LCSW Consulting P.C. and is an adjunct professor and field advisor at Fordham University's MSW Program.

Madeline has dedicated her career to seeking to improve systems and organizations that work with and service people. As a social work professor and consultant, she trains students and professionals on how to work within the current mental health system with less stress and burnout. Madeline believes in teaching and empowering her clients to be their own therapists and advocates. She confronts problems with teamwork and solution focused strategies. Kindness and humor are her trademark.

Madeline has a master's degree from New York University Silver School of Social Work and a bachelor's degree in psychology from Hunter College of CUNY. She is bilingual in Spanish. Madeline lives in Westchester County, NY with her dog Moofasah and cat Poombah. She is currently in plans to open a clinic practice in NYC providing psychotherapy for Latino and African American children and families and autism evaluation services.

Madeline Maldonado
madeline.maldonadolcswr@gmail.com
IG:@latinacsw
LinkedIn: mmaldonado-lcswr/

LEAD OTHERS, THEN LEAD YOURSELF

YURILKA A. HERNANDEZ, LCSW

My name is Yurilka Hernandez, and I am an Afro-Latina from the Dominican Republic. I want to share my journey and how I am navigating my Latinidad in the social work world. As a first-generation Latina, I have achieved more than I expected. I would like to say that one of my more distinguished characteristics is that I have a very heavy accent, something that I struggled with until I met the real leaders of my community.

ONE OF OUR OWN

I was sixteen when I first moved to the United States of America. I remember it like it was yesterday. It was December 1st, 2004. I was immediately re-enrolled in high school, and it was in there where I experienced micro-aggressions and discrimination by one of our own. She was the school counselor, a Latina from Puerto Rico who advised me to drop out and take the GED, because I did not speak or write in English and I was not going to be able to pass the English state exam in 6 months.

I considered this option for like five minutes because she was there to help, or so I thought. However, I have never been one to listen to people who tell me, "You are not capable of archiving." I was already dealing with culture shock from being at a school that looked like a prison. Previously, I went to a beautiful school in DR and I did not like the cage-like feeling, where the students had to go through a metal detector every time you walked into school—and not even cell phones were allowed.

When I was in Dominican Republic, my school was in an open field. We ate lunch outside in the grass, and it was incredibly beautiful. I never knew how much that grass meant to me, until I was sitting in a cafeteria room full of kids and some police officers were walking around. Between that and a counselor telling me I was not going to make it, I was full of doubt and fear—but I decided to raise up anyway.

MAMI, PAPI Y EL APOYO

My parents are the most amazing humans I know. They have supported me, encouraged me, driven me to all my awards, and never complained about taking time off to be there. My mother, who is the most supportive and amazing woman I know, always told me that I was lucky. Lucky for people to like me, to connect with me, and invest. She has always been my biggest supporter, my number one fan and biggest role model. My mother values time management, follow ups, and accountability, values that I benefit in my personal and professional life. Every time I made an honor roll, for the minimal recognition I got, my mother has always been there.

THE AMERIKAA DREAM

I was nineteen when I found out that I could go to college and receive financial assistance. I enrolled in Bronx Community College to become a lawyer. While I was in BCC, I took a liberal class, and it was a human services introduction. It was an elective. It was supposed to be an easy class, but I never suspected that this class was going to change my life. I debated ideas, topics, and fought for my views with classmates and professors. By the time I realized I had taken all my classes in human services, I had to declare a major, so I changed it from law to human services. It was there in my final semester that I met a professor who after I argued with for hours in class about the topic of equality, human rights, poverty, and other things, he offered me an internship at his full-time placement. I was overly excited about this opportunity, because I heard so much about inequality, poverty, drug use, and so many human rights issues that I just could not believe that we had so much to advocate for.

SOCIAL WORK: THE TREE OF LIFE

I showed up exceedingly early that first the morning, ready to start my internship. I was twenty. I remember when I walked in that shelter it was dark and cloudy. Everybody had a room that looked like a classic advertising for hopelessness. The population that was being served there was the HIV population, and although it was 2007, they looked like early eighties.

It took a while for me to tell my family I was treating people with HIV because of the stigma that surrounded the Latino community around HIV. I took the first step of removing stigma, I educated my family, and promoted change.

I interned with my professor for a year, then he hired me. This is when I learned how much paper goes into social work, the endless notes.

Since I had already graduated with my associate's degree, shortly after, I got another job at another nonprofit organization. I was there for four years when I inquired about a leadership position. I was told I need a higher degree, therefore I decided to go back to school, because I wanted to lead, since in these organizations there were no leaders that represented *me*. I enrolled in Lehman College for my bachelor's degree, and it was the best thing I ever did. There I met some wonderful women who today are family. Lehman is very diverse, and I never felt alone or like an outsider. I had some incredible people that only inspired me to do better and supported me. For this reason, I applied to NYU for my master's program.

THE LONELY LIONESS

NYU and I have a special relationship; this is the school that I chose, that I researched, and it is a school that I was so passionate about. They had so much to offer me, so in April 2014 when I had my acceptance letter from NYU, it changed my life.

I was beyond thrilled; I could not believe that just ten years prior I actually considered dropping out of high school because I did not speak a language good enough for me to get into such a school. My experience at NYU gave me unique perspective; and unlike Lehman, where every room had someone like me, that sounded like me, look like me, here there was nobody. There were no Afro-Latinos, no culture, no professors. So we tried to create a club, and it was only seven of us from different departments. It was not successful, but in 2017, another group of Latinos came and built something beautiful. In May 2015, I became a master social worker, while my two very Dominican parents cheered on from the balcony of the Lincoln Center.

THE DIAMOND IN THE ROUGH, BORN TO LEAD

May 5th, 2015, I got an interview to work for Acacia Networks, and here is where my real journey began. I had never heard of them before, but I did my research and I learned that they were the second largest nonprofit organization in New York City. It was not until I walked into this interview that I met the one who would become one of the most influential persons in my professional life. I met Mrs. Yaberci Perez-Cubilla, a tall brunette Dominican woman who sat across from me, very elegant, as she told me that she was taking over a new location in the Bronx and she was looking for hardworking, motivated people who were not afraid to work in an amazingly fast paced environment. At this point she could have told me that I was going to be frying *platanos* in the corner and I will have said yes. I had worked for many other organizations before, and none of their leadership looked like me.

These phenomenally successful companies did not look like me, they did not speak like me, they did not sound like me, they did not come from where I came from, and although at the time she was only a program director, I was very impressed.

Fast forward seven years later, and I am sitting in her chair today. She has opened doors for me, she has pushed me to be better, she has put her faith in me, she trusted me—and I can never repay that. Over the years, we developed a relationship, and although she won't admit it, she is my mentor.

REPRESENTATION MATTERS

I worked at this company for a long time. Most people always ask me, "Why do you stay there? Why don't you move right away?" I will tell you why: I could go to any place I want; I have my license and I got everything that I wanted to get; my goals have been met professionally, as I have embarked in many different adventures. But Acacia Network has allowed me to do all that and more.

Professional growth is one of the most important things for me, and Acacia Network has allowed me to grow professionally. They have invested in my career, and that is one of the most important things to find in an agency as big as this one.

Throughout the years, I have seen extraordinarily strong

women like Lymaris, who for me has become a great inspiration. She came into a meeting we were having and shared her story with us, about how she decided to move from Puerto Rico to pursue her career goals, and today she leads the largest nonprofit organization. She is a leader who looks, speaks, and has an accent like me.

LEADING MYSELF WITH AN ARMY NEXT TO ME

I want to inspire women. I recognize how far I have gotten in life by working hard, and despite having a heavy accent like I do, when I speak, there is no fear; there is no embarrassment, there is no questioning myself: I am powerful. I learned a long time ago that having people that look like you in the field in leadership positions makes so much of a difference.

Today I am fearless and bold, with my heavy accent, unapologetic salt and pepper hair that continues pushing boundaries, faithful to my dreams and a hunger for success. I have learned that you can accomplish anything that you want if you have the right people supporting you. I no longer apologize for being ambitious, for being loud, for dreaming beyond expectations. It is remarkable for me to be able to work like I do, encourage, and help the new generation of social workers to be better and to be bigger. As a woman, daughter, sister, auntie, friend, social worker, teacher and practitioner, representation matters.

REFLECTION

It's always important to remember to come back to your roots if you ever feel lost. Self-care is a priority no matter what stage of your life you are in. Working out provides me with great solace, and weight lifting and Crossfit training are my passion and provide me great relief. By keeping my body as active as my mind, I get to work through emotions and keep them in check.

ABOUT THE AUTHOR

Yurilka Hernandez is a Licensed Clinical Social Worker in the state of New York (LCSW). She is the CEO and founder of Psychotherapy & Consultation Services LCSW-PLLC. She is a bilingual, bi-cultural Hispanic female with over thirteen years of extensive training and experience in the areas of mental health, cultural competency, working with immigrant families, substance abuse disorders and providing clinical supervision.

Her educational background includes a Bachelor of Science and a graduate degree (MSW) from New York University Silver School of Social Work. In 2016, she completed a Post-Master's Certificate Program in psychoanalytic psychotherapy from Manhattan Institute for Psychoanalysis, and certified middle management from the National Council for Behavioral Health 2019, and Executive Leadership for Nonprofit Organization at New York University.

As part of the behavior Team at Acacia Network, the second largest Latino led not –for- profit organization in the country, her portfolio includes mental health clinics, substance abuse school-based programs, court involved youth programs and health homes.

As a field supervisor and teacher at Adelphi university school of social work, she has cultivated healthy and positive relationships with students by shaping our next line of social workers with their journey.

Today Yurilka works as a senior administrator for health homes. She also participates in multiple advocacies in Washington, D.C. and Albany where she fights for her patients, fellow social workers, and the well-being of others.

She is a daughter, sister, friend, lover, and ally. She fights every day for social justice, while promoting growth and hope. Social work is the tree of life and she is a messenger!

Yurilka A. Hernandez

psychotherapy-today.com

PUSHING THROUGH ADVERSITY

INGRID MCFARLANE, MSW, LCSW-R

UNA MESCLA

I firmly believe that social work was a natural progression of my life story. From incredibly early on, I became acutely aware about how race, color, and ethnicity impacted my life. I was born in Brooklyn, New York, but raised initially internationally in London, England. I would spend summers in New York until I moved back to Queens, New York, the summer prior to starting sixth grade.

My family wanted to expose me to all different races and ethnicities. As a result, I attended private Catholic schools from kindergarten through twelfth grade. The common denominator between myself and my classmates was the Catholic religion. There was a slim minority of students who were not Roman Catholic (i.e., Greek Orthodox, Hinduism, etc.) in middle school. In the all-girl private school that I attended, The Mary Louis

Academy, I was exposed to students with much more diverse religions.

While I lived in London, I was aware of the differences in race between me and my classmates. However, everyone was very accepting, to the point that there was a great deal of interracial dating. It was not until I moved back permanently to New York and started sixth grade that I became aware of my differences in relation to the other students in a negative manner.

I am an Afro-Latina, with my maternal grandmother being from Cuba. As many people from Latino or Latinx background are aware, what makes us beautiful is that physically we can have diverse features, people from "una mescla," a mixture of someone from a European background and African background, from Indian or Asian backgrounds, European backgrounds, or primarily African background.

DO YOU SEE ME?

My physical characteristics (like skin tone and hair texture) appear to be of someone of African descent. It is only when I speak in Spanish that people then assume that I am of Dominican descent.

When I was growing up in the 1980s and 1990s, anyone who was not of European descent in the United States was considered a "minority." As pejorative as the term "minority" appeared to be, I felt smaller and more insignificant than I had ever felt in my young life. Other students would tease me about my hair worn in braids, calling the braids "train tracks" and would make fun of me.

I also noticed that the teachers did not always hear me or notice me when I would raise my hand to participate in class. Despite being ignored, I was always an exceptionally good student. So, I was very taken aback by the fact that I was not getting the recognition that I would usually have received for my grades in London. I noticed that my Caucasian friends were treated differently than me.

When I went to high school, I went to an all-girl Catholic high school, which was very prestigious. I am so thankful for the education that I received at this school. However, I feel that because of my race and ethnicity, I was not encouraged to succeed the way that my Caucasian classmates were. I excelled in my classes and took the PSAT examination in my sophomore year, I scored extremely high, and was awarded a National Merit Scholarship Award. My academic achievement made me so proud! The reaction I received from my high school was very sedated, to say the least. There were two other students of color who had also achieved high scores on the PSAT. One student was Afro-Panamanian American and the other was African American. The school did not give the recognition for having students in their school achieve high scores on a national examination. In addition, there was no encouragement from teachers or school administration to keep up the excellent work to get into a college or university of our choosing.

LOVE THYSELF

It became clear to me that my physical appearance, race, and ethnicity played a crucial role in how people responded to me. I knew that I had to try harder than Caucasian students to stand out and receive recognition for accomplishments.

As I entered Sarah Lawrence College, I was blessed with a school that welcomed students, learning about their race, ethnicity, and culture, and encouraged pride. My professors were also multi-racially diverse. As a result, I had faces of professors, both male and female, who looked like me and understood the issues facing people from Latino and African American cultures.

It was at this time that I started to feel more comfortable in my skin, and realized that I did not have to feel that there was something wrong with me because my complexion was darker, my hair was not naturally straight, my lips were fuller, and my physical features were not typical European features. One of my professors and mentors also saw the change in me, introduced me to the profession of social work, and encouraged me to apply a graduate degree program.

My professor's alma mater was the University of Pennsylvania. So, he encouraged me to apply there as my first choice for a social work graduate program. I applied and was accepted into University of Pennsylvania School of Social Policy and Practice with a partial tuition scholarship. This was the beginning of my connection to social justice initiatives.

My time at the University of Pennsylvania taught me about myself and the issues in the world that I wanted to change. My first year in the graduate program, I joined social clubs that helped me to connect and network with other Afro-Latina students. This continued to help shape my identity as a person of color, and highlighted for me many of the issues facing Afro Latinos. My first year internship was in the Division of Juvenile Justice and was able to work with many incarcerated young people who were of African American backgrounds and Latino backgrounds.

SOCIAL JUSTICE WARRIOR

In my second and final year at the University of Pennsylvania, I finally found my niche. Initially, I thought that I would pursue a dual master's degree in social work and the Juris Doctor program to work with African Americans and Latinos as a public defender in the court system. However, as I started my second year internship at the Children's Seashore House of the Children's Hospital of Philadelphia, it became clear that my impact would be in healthcare.

I was introduced to many different medical and mental health diagnoses and the treatments necessary for cure or management of these illnesses. This was exciting, and I learned a great deal. However, it also highlighted for me the health disparities that exist amongst African American and Latino patients. Moreover, this internship introduced me to social determinants of healthcare.

PASSIONATE SOCIAL CHANGE AGENT

With this newfound knowledge, I decided to focus my

master's thesis on the impact of race, ethnicity, gender, religion, and socioeconomics on healthcare in children with chronic illnesses. I used both quantitative and qualitative data in my research. To perform my investigation, I interviewed members of the interdisciplinary healthcare team to get their thoughts on race, gender, religion, and socioeconomic background, and how this impacted how they cared for their patients. In addition, I brought in different speakers to give talks on the impact of race, religion, and socioeconomic backgrounds on patients prior to them coming to the healthcare system, and how these experiences shape the way that they respond to members of the healthcare team and medicine.

I also conducted surveys with patients/family members. Throughout this process, I learned so much about myself and the impact that I could have on social justice. Since I am fluent in Spanish and French, I was able to connect with patients/family members who had Limited English proficiency, and could hear the way that seeking healthcare in a language different from their own made them feel alienated, alone, and helpless to protect their children.

As I was getting closer to graduating, I began my job hunt, and knew that I wanted to work in healthcare and continue to assist patients/families from these diverse backgrounds. At the Children's Hospital of Philadelphia, I was amongst many fellow University of Pennsylvania students who were also interns.

I was offered a job at a nursing home at the end of the interview. With this exciting news, I came back to tell the director of social work that I had received a job at the nursing home after my interview, and I was so excited that I would have a job upon graduation. I had taken my licensure examination the week before and had passed it. So, I was able to start work as soon as my degree was conferred. The director of social work looked me in the eye and said, "Ingrid, it will be such a waste for you to work in a nursing home with the elderly! You have so much energy, enthusiasm, and a great spirit. I believe that you should continue to work with children." I was then offered the job as the Cerebral Palsy Social Worker and Tracheotomy and Ventilation Unit Social Worker at The Children's Seashore House of the Children's Hospital of Philadelphia and I accepted the position. That was how I started my career in healthcare as a social justice advocate.

PUSHING THE DOORS OPEN

My director at The Children's Hospital of Philadelphia allowed me to give cultural competency presentations to new hires during their orientation period. As a result, I was able to highlight the issues that many of these healthcare workers who may have not been aware of the interplay of race, gender, socioeconomic status, religion, and ethnicity can play in the healthcare system, and I was also able to highlight the social determinants of healthcare. I was also able to work on the hospital's Family Handbook and ensure that there were translations in Spanish and French. As a social worker, I worked with limited English proficiency patients and their families, and provided interpretation at family/team meetings, and during health discussions to ensure that they understood the medical information in their primary language. Being an Afro-Latina, I was also able to help to assure patients that their concerns and needs were being listened to and addressed, and that they did not have to feel embarrassed to discuss their concerns with me.

When I returned to New York, I started working in the Northwell Health System in the Division of Child Adolescent Psychiatry. I became familiar with the impact of mental health and the fact that it was just as important as addressing your physical health needs. Working in an onsite school program in Astoria, New York, I provided individual, group, and family therapy to students who were primarily from Latino, African American, and Afro-Caribbean backgrounds.

In my current position, I work with pediatric cancer patients and their families at Cohen Children's Medical Center in the division of hematology/oncology. I am assigned to patients/families who speak primarily Spanish and French. In order to provide greater advocacy, I also work on the Family Advisory Council with hospital administration and parents/caregivers to make the hospital policies and practices more patient/family centered and culturally humble.

SOCIAL WORK LEGACY

I believe that my legacy in social work will be that I am an unapologetic social change advocate. I constantly fight to ensure that patients of diverse backgrounds have a voice, their concerns are heard by people who can make a change, and that their needs can and will be addressed. I passionately believe that by highlighting the importance of hiring diverse healthcare staff to represent the patient population, we can dramatically decrease healthcare disparities.

Every Latina needs drive to succeed. Never give up on your dreams and your passions. What drives you is what is going to bring you fulfillment. Once you have found your niche, you can make an impact because of that driving spirit. I believe that we can amplify other Latinas by opening the doors to opportunities whenever you are able to do so for the next person.

In addition, giving guidance and mentorship to the next generation of Latina social workers is a valuable tool. Tell them your pitfalls, so that they will not repeat them. Provide them with your pearls of wisdom. Other social work professionals need this book so that they can continue their advocacy work. Social work is an incredibly challenging profession. We are a helping profession. However, we must also help ourselves to meet the challenges of our client population.

Most people admire the fact that I do not give up when there are challenging cases that I am faced with, and that these cases invigorate me. I became this way because I had to fight through life academically, professionally, and personally, through many hardships and adversities.

The most difficult personal issue that I have had to face has been coping with the loss of my first-born son, Brad, in 2018 due to a sudden cardiac death. This was and is the worst thing that can happen to any parent. For me, it was as if the air and life had been sucked out of me. One day my son was alive and well, and the next morning he was gone from a cardiac issue that no one saw coming. My entire world was turned upside down. I was grieving for the loss of my first-born son, and scared about how this would affect my younger son, Jordan. My faith has helped me as I continue to heal each day. As ironic as it may sound, helping others in need has helped me to continue to heal.

REFLECTION

1. What is the biggest challenge that you have faced in your life?

2. What have you found to be an anchor when you are facing these challenges (i.e. your family, your partner, your faith, etc.)?

3. As you have overcome obstacles in your life, has that helped you to feel better equipped to face other challenges?

ABOUT THE AUTHOR

Ingrid received her master's degree in social work from the University of Pennsylvania School of Social Policy and Practice. She is a licensed clinical social worker with the "R" psychotherapy privilege in the state of New York. Ingrid is currently employed as a pediatric oncology social worker in the Northwell Health system at Cohen Children's Medical Center of New York. In addition, Ingrid has a private practice working with children, adolescents, individuals, and couples in Huntington, NY.

Her clinical experience is across a variety of settings, and includes inpatient and outpatient specialty clinics, crisis intervention, school mental health alliance, child and adolescent psychiatry, traumatic brain injury, Neuro rehabilitation, physical medicine and rehabilitation, hematology/oncology, neonatal and pediatric intensive care, and emergency medicine and trauma.

Embracing her passion for group work, Ingrid has also led parent support groups for the caregivers of children with a variety of oncological diagnoses and teen groups focusing on anger management and coping skills. She has also provided clinical and administrative supervision to undergraduate and graduate social work interns and professionals. Ingrid is passionate about providing therapeutic services to individuals and groups in crisis in a culturally humble manner focusing on BIPOC and immigrant populations.

Ingrid is trilingual and can speak, read, and write in English, Spanish, and French fluently. As a result, Ingrid is passionate about providing therapy in the client's primary language to ensure that she embraces the full cultural identity of her clients as she utilizes a holistic, strength based, person centered approach to guide her practice. She utilizes a variety of techniques and skills drawn from recognized therapeutic models including Cognitive Behavioral Therapy, Solution Focused, Psychoeducation, Play Therapy, Motivational Interviewing, and Family Systems Therapy.

Ingrid received The Cohen Children's Medical Center's Patient/Customer Focus Award in February 2020. Erica Sandoval, MSW, LCSW, president of the NASW-NY chapter and Ingrid will be launching "E & I Consulting" in 2022.

Ingrid McFarlane, MSW, LCSW-R
ingridmcfarlanelcswr@gmail.com
516-986-7560

Madrina

MORE THAN ENOUGH

DR. LINDA LAUSELL BRYANT, MSW, PH.D.

"Honoring who I came from while confronting thought patterns that need change."

BELIEVING WHAT YOU CAN'T SEE

"Ay, ahí está'!" ("There he is!") Grandma exclaimed, shaking off a slight tremor from being startled. "Who?" "Where?" I asked. I was six, and not yet able to understand that grandma saw things that I could not see. "El Doctor" (The Doctor) she said. She was referring to a vision she saw of a man wearing a white coat and carrying a satchel, like a doctor. "I don't see him," I said, wondering how she could see him. She told me that he was often with me, accompanying me, guiding me. I could not see him, but it felt good to know that a doctor was invisibly watching over me and that according to my grandmother, he was a good guide.

Social work aims to understand people in the context of their social environment. When I think about the environments that have shaped me, it is no surprise that social work is my career choice, and such a foundational part of who I am. It is part of my professional and personal identity. It is my vocation and avocation.

The profession's values are ingrained in my purpose: pursuing, social justice, respecting the dignity and worth of each individual, centering the importance of relationships and practicing with integrity and competence. In the thirty-five years of my career to date, I have aimed to 'see' others with more than what meets the natural eye; to see their strengths, gifts, and talents as well as their pain. I aim to be a mirror that reflects their strengths, to listen for what is said and unsaid. "I see you." "I hear you."

Being seen and heard is a gift that affirms the humanity in each of us. Far too many go through life feeling unseen and unheard, feeling invisible. My mind goes to immigrants, refugees, teens of color, and others who have gotten the message that they do not matter enough to be seen or heard, whether in the workplace, a restaurant, or by policies that determine their level of access to the things that all humans need. Each of us can give the gift of seeing and hearing others. We can use whatever position or privilege we may have to insist that we all should be seen and heard, because we all have dignity and worth.

SIEMPRE CONMIGO (ALWAYS WITH ME)

My identity as a social worker predates any formal training I received. Reflecting on how it developed and emerged, my mind goes to my grandmother. Each of my grandparents came from Puerto Rico as teenagers, arriving with barely a dollar in their pockets but with a fistful of dreams. Arriving in New York City as a teenage girl in the late 1920s, my grandmother, Candita Valentin, had known poverty and hardship. She experienced the routine discrimination directed at new immigrants, including brown-skinned people from Puerto Rico. She had a strong sense of herself as a respectable, virtuous, hardworking person of dignity and like many immigrants, thought that who she was would help her transcend those stereotypes.

She worked doing sewing, domestic work, and later, factory work. She met my grandpa, Gilberto Rosado, and they married, having seven children. My mother was the fourth child. They were tough disciplinarians, and Grandma worried about keeping her three daughters safe, so they could leave her home one day as brides, 'properly' married. She wanted her sons to be good men and good providers for the families they'd have one day. My grandpa wanted them to be men's men, strong, tough, hard working.

All the girls were loyal and devoted to their mother and didn't dream of disappointing her. They all graduated from high school and married 'properly' in church. These markers of respectability and success were very important to my grandparents. They were well-aware of the way immigrants like them were viewed and talked about. With the growing number of Puerto Ricans coming to NYC, they experienced the prejudiced attitudes and stereotypes about them having lots of kids or being loud or lazy. They set out to establish that they were respectable, dignified people who raised their children with good values.

As members of a community that was not held in high regard, I watched my grandmother take great care of people in her community. She served as a social worker for her community. Doña Candita, as she was known by the community, was an MSW in her own right and in her own sense.

She was a minister, a sage, and a warrior. Her community sought her for her warm and welcoming demeanor, her wise counsel, and the generosity with which she shared her resources, however limited. She would not hesitate to pull a change purse out of her bra and share a dollar or two, or to pack up a plate of food, to offer a prayer and a blessing. She would not hesitate to accompany someone to an important appointment for support. She could not translate or intercede formally, but she could be with them in solidarity, and she could pray and lend her emotional strength and support of the person in need.

She affirmed others and their capacity to triumph over adversity. "Tú vas a tener éxito" she would declare. "Ten fe." "Todo va a salir bien." (You will succeed; have faith. Everything will work out). My grandmother modeled perseverance and triumph over adversity, even if the triumph was to survive a lifetime of suffering and adversity. As she would say, "Hay que cargar la cruz, como hizo el santísimo Jesús." ("We have to bear our cross, as Jesus did.").

She was unapologetically Latina, though she understood that she and other Puerto Ricans were viewed in a manner that was a distortion from who we really were. Her attitude was that we knew who we were and that's what mattered. We should do our best to rise above it all. Her faith shaped her orientation as well. She focused on pleasing a higher power, and it helped her put people with social and economic power in perspective.

My mother, Josephine Rosado, was a strong, determined woman who found it difficult to ignore what others thought of her and of us as a people. She was determined to prove that she was as good as those who looked down on us, maybe even better. She was always striving, pushing to reach levels that exceeded grandma and grandpa's humble lives, all the while striving to make them proud and bring them up several levels with her own achievements.

She worked to live a life that was above reproach. She put a lot of pressure on herself to succeed, and achieved many of the markers of success for a young woman in the 1950s: She graduated high school, got a 'good' job at a life insurance company, and didn't date until after high school graduation, complying with my grandparents' strict standards. She helped her parents financially with her salary and at the age of twenty-four, married Damian Caso Lausell, a man that they approved of.

She was a devoted mother, and enrolled me in one of the early cohorts of Head Start. She was hired to work as a paraprofessional teacher in my elementary school. I watched her encourage, teach, and push students from our community to do well, to live up to their potential, and to represent our culture with pride and distinction. She pushed me to do the same, and was proud of how much I loved school and how well I did. My mother's fury at the prejudice and discrimination directed at Puerto Ricans expressed itself in her passionate advocacy for others. She would help family and friends navigate systems, making phone calls or helping them write letters. When there was a problem, the family knew to call Josie. She was hired as a paralegal in a law firm in the 1980s and I watched her advocate for Latinx clients to be treated fairly.

My story is incomplete without acknowledging the role that my father played in my life. He had a very tough life growing up with a level of poverty that meant a daily meal was not a given. He only achieved an eighth grade education in Puerto Rico, so that he could pursue steady work. Damian Caso Lausell was a self-taught man, reading everything he could and developing his own philosophies on just about everything. He would preach that we should investigate, analyze, validate, and verify everything. I think he influenced my intellectual curiosity and love of learning. He was fiercely proud of being Puerto Rican, and when he retired from his career as a merchant marine, he moved us to Puerto Rico to live. He may have only had an eighth grade education, but he had a Ph.D. in Life.

STOP AUDITIONING: YOU GOT THE PART!

I loved school and I loved learning, but I had internalized the pressure to be above reproach, to be perfect in as many ways as possible. Upon reflection, I realize that my grandmother's pride in our culture was unshaken, unapologetic. She coped with the discrimination, but did not seem to internalize it. On the other hand, the stress really affected her, and she suffered from heart disease. My mother was inwardly defiant but externally compliant. It infuriated her that people looked down at Puerto Ricans, and she also felt and acted on the pressure to give them nothing negative to talk about.

These two amazing Latina women were so influential in my life, and so was my father. On a positive level, I was encouraged to be the best I could and to achieve, and yet an unintended consequence was a nagging sense that I could never let up, never relax. I would always need to do more.

This evolved into a host of achievements throughout my life. I was the valedictorian in my high school in Puerto Rico, skipping two grades and graduating at sixteen. At twenty, I became the first college graduate in our family. I got my first social work job at twenty-two, as a caseplanner for the Children's Aid Society, and by twenty-six, I had my MSW.

I was a program director at the Children's Aid Society in my twenties. In my thirties, I was a division director at Victim Services and an assistant executive director at the Partnership for After School Education. In my forties, I was an associate commissioner at NYC's Administration for Children's Services, and executive director of Inwood House.

I have been interviewed on television and in print media related to my work. I achieved my Ph. D in social work in 2012. I joined the faculty at NYU Silver School of Social Work in 2015, and will now be directing their Doctorate in Social Work program. I have co-authored two books and several articles and have been acknowledged with a Lifetime Achievement Award by the Latino Social Work Coalition and Scholarship Fund. I have worked to raise hundreds of thousands of dollars to launch an adaptive leadership initiative for social work students at NYU Silver and, and, and… I am exhausted.

I have been recognized professionally and academically. Every opportunity came with the pressure of an audition, and even when I 'got the part', in my mind, the audition did not end. Every victory came at a cost—to my health and my peace of mind.

It feels like it is never enough; no matter what I achieve, I am never done proving myself. I cannot rest. Taking care of myself feels like a luxury meant for others but not for me. For me, it is self-indulgence or worse, laziness. I have had a career in social work marked by high achievement and dedicated service, and burnout is a constant companion.

Today, I can look at my thirty-five years in the field of social work with pride, but I have many big lessons left to learn. I realize that I have been in the grip of an oppressed mindset. I need to learn how to work to live rather than living to work. I want to live Audrey Lorde's message that "Caring for myself is not self-indulgence, it is self-preservation, and that is an act of political warfare."

WRESTLING WITH THE OPPRESSOR WITHIN

"Political warfare" is a charged term, and a necessity for

people who are in a constant struggle for equity, for our humanity to be acknowledged. I understand the need for it, since the struggle continues, no matter what we may have collectively proven. I have embraced this fight as core to my purpose.

As I fight these external forces, one of my biggest struggles is to care for myself, and I have a number of health challenges as sad trophies of this. I need to internalize that someone else's opinion of me is not what makes me good. I am enough. Our ancestors did what they needed to do to survive the hostilities they faced, so that we would have the opportunities we did. Now, I can share my struggle and take in the strength of their and my hard-earned wisdom. I can stay connected to my community, and recognize that I am enough, just as I am. I need not 'prove' that to anyone. Caring for ourselves is fundamental to social justice. We cannot fight external oppressors while oppressing ourselves.

Knowing this intellectually is one thing. Putting it into practice is a whole other struggle. While this is my personal struggle and challenge, it isn't unique to me. Our profession is also complicit. The social work profession has thrived on this ethos of selflessness, devotion, and dedication, coming from our caring and the expectation that we can do this most challenging of transformative work on the sheer power of our good will, our deep caring and concern, without adequate compensation or resources needed for the work. We have glorified such levels of self-sacrifice in this woman-dominated profession. It is unacceptable. It is exploitative. It must change, and we will change it.

REFLECTION

At this point in my life and career, I want to focus on these deep issues of internalized race-based oppression that impact individuals and generations. I hope my legacy will include the tradition of 'levantando', of rising to lift up others. My individual success is necessary but not sufficient. I don't want to be an exception. I want to contribute to success being the norm for our people, people of color. That is why I have been committed to mentoring and supporting the next generations. I hope my legacy will be "que sí se puede—pero nunca a solas, siempre con apoyo". "Yes, we can, but not alone, always with support."

My beautiful and brilliant daughter Jasmine is going into the field of social work, and I hope that she and all the future generations of social workers will challenge our profession's practice of normalizing exploitative levels of self-sacrifice in the name of service.

I can use every platform I've worked so hard for to lift up Latinx and all people of color—a "nosotros" orientation. 'Nosotros' is the essence of what it means to me to be Latinx in social work.

- How do your internal oppressors manifest in your professional life?
- Do you have some 'sad trophies' from your journey?
- How are you doing with moving past the 'audition' process and 'owning the part?'

ABOUT THE AUTHOR

Dr. Linda Lausell Bryant is clinical associate professor, director of the doctorate in social work program, and the Katherine and Howard Aibel Executive-in-Residence at NYU Silver. She is devoted to developing the leadership capacities of social workers for impact on the pressing social issues of our time, the intersection of race, ethnicity, and social justice, child welfare issues, and macro social work practice.

Dr. Lausell Bryant's career spans thirty-five years in youth services in both the private and public sectors. She has launched an Adaptive Leadership in Human Services Institute at NYU Silver, served as the executive director of Inwood House, a nonprofit youth agency from 2005-2014, and served as associate commissioner for the Office of Youth Development at the NYC Administration for Children's Services. She served on the NYC Panel for Education Policy and currently serves as the president of the board of the National Crittenton Foundation, which seeks to empower young women and girls. She received the 2021 Lifetime Achievement Award from the Latino Social Work Coalition and has received the Distinguished Contribution to Student Engagement Award at NYU Silver. She is the co-author of "A Guide for Sustaining Conversations on Racism, Identity and Our Mutual Humanity" and *Social Work: A Call to Action.*

Linda Lausell Bryant
drlindarenews@gmail.com
Linked in: Dr. Linda Lausell Bryant

IT CAN GET BETTER

TANIA VARGAS, LCSW

Knowing who you are is a lifelong learning process. What do I want to be when I grow up? What will I look like? Where will I live? All of these questions and so many more were always running through my head throughout most of my childhood and adolescence. My hometown felt too small, and a bit too racist, so I wanted to be almost anywhere else.

I wanted to be so many different things when I grew up; the two most consistent careers were being a lawyer or a photographer. I have always been artistic and enjoyed photography greatly. I had a camera since middle school and was the child always taking photos. This gave me a sense of belonging and purpose because people wanted me around to capture those moments. I was needed—and it was a great feeling.

IT ALMOST ALWAYS STARTS DURING CHILDHOOD

Growing up, many of the instances of teasing and bullying were due to my weight. For me, this almost pushed my identity of being a first-generation Mexican American to the side. I didn't feel different because I was Mexican; I felt different because I was fat. I was almost always surrounded by White people, and I would forget that I was not the same and that my family had a completely different life compared to that of my peers. In many situations where I was the only person of color, someone would say or do something that would bring me back to the reality that I could never be 100% like the rest of the group. It felt confusing and almost degrading at times, and I never knew how to properly respond to those situations.

As I got older, while I was still fat, my race became more prominent in my life. I was being reminded all the time that I was not like everyone else and that I didn't fully belong. This was happening at my school, in random stores, and also at my church. It was hard to navigate my identity, and I felt like I constantly had to prove my worth. It was exhausting.

THE TURNING POINT

My junior year in high school was my rock bottom. I had been in an emotionally abusive relationship that summer and ended up being assaulted and nearly strangled to death by someone I really loved at the time. I had put my family in harm's way that night as well, and it caused such a rift between us all. It was a night that changed the course of my life.

I was put into therapy in hopes to make me "better." I did not think it would help, but I also knew I had no choice in the matter. It took me a few years to truly realize it, but this therapist changed my life. She helped guide me into repairing my relationship with my parents and brothers and gave me the encouragement to take charge of my life—and to figure out what I wanted to do with it.

Going to therapy gave me a guided hand as I started my senior year of high school. I still loved photography and thought art school would be the way to go. I was accepted into a small art school and got a small scholarship too!

I remember the night that I told my dad about the scholarship. He looked at me with such a straight face and said this money was basically worthless, and I should not go. I was crushed. My father told me that night that I needed to pick a field where I would make money and that I could do photography as a hobby. The medical field seemed like the smart way to go. This also played into showing everyone else my worth, and that I could be in a respectable field, make a good financial living for myself, and that I was a necessity in my community.

GETTING OLDER, TRYING TO GET WISER

I had been accepted into a respiratory care two-year program and was thrilled with the knowledge that I would be done with school and could start working before my peers. I was eighteen on my first day of college. When I sat down, I quickly noticed that everyone was significantly older than me.

A few women, who ended up being from India, sat near me and started to chat with me. They were surprised to see someone so young in the program and asked why I wanted to be a respiratory therapist. Then "those" questions started: *Where are you from? Where is your family from? Oh, you're Mexican? But you have so many Indian features.* I knew they meant well, but in that moment, it was clear that they talked to me because they thought they could relate to me. After that day, they didn't talk to me socially for the rest of the semester.

Ultimately, this program was not for me, and I was let go after my first semester. I recommend not joining a medical program if you have never ever taken a human anatomy class before. There was also a lot more math than I had realized, which was never a strong skill of mine.

It took me a while to tell my parents I was kicked out of the program. This came from a place of shame but, also, I wanted a plan. I felt it would have been easier for my parents to hear that I was kicked out of the program if I already knew what I was going to do next. The truth was, I had no idea what I wanted to do. I took my general education classes and started looking at other majors. I needed to find a career that I could fall in love with.

THE POINT OF SELF DISCOVERY

At this point, I had lost touch with a good portion of my "best friends" in high school and my high school sweetheart and I had ended our relationship. I felt so alone, and I was not sure how to make new friends in college. I had gone to the same church for most of my life, and they sponsored a college ministry at the nearby university, so I thought that was my best bet of making new friends. I was right.

I ended up meeting my best friend at the first event I

attended. He was super cool, and clearly the life of the party. He was so kind and quickly made friends with everyone around him. We exchanged numbers and started hanging out a lot more. He was a social work major, and he started talking to me more about the program. I also started talking to other people who were majoring in social work as well.

Growing up, all I really knew about social work was that they were child protective workers and took away abused children. The more I learned about the program, the more I fell in love with it. Social work was way more than being part of child protective services. Social workers could be almost everywhere because the need to help people was always there. I started taking classes to ensure that I could immediately join the program when I graduated with my associate's degree. This was my only plan, the only school I applied to. I was so nervous waiting for that application decision. Did I make a huge mistake only applying for one school? What would happen if I didn't get in? What else could I do?

But I got in! I sobbed for several minutes reading that acceptance email. The first day of my classes felt so different from any of my other college courses. Everyone had such an inviting presence, and while I was nervous, I didn't feel like I was out of place. It felt good to find a place where I almost automatically felt like I needed to be there. It all further affirmed that this was something that I could do for the rest of my life.

All of my classes revolved around advocating, active listening, and not taking away power from those we are supposed to serve. All these points were made stronger by us talking about ourselves, talking about any type of trauma we had gone through, how our identities shaped us, and how to further shape ourselves. Many of my classes gave me the space to talk about my life and my experiences in an authentic and genuine way. I did not feel like I had to put on a show or had to make up excuses for some of the things that had happened to me. I could share what I wanted, and when I cried, I was met with compassion and empathy.

REDEFINING WHO I AM

Along with learning more about myself and the issues I needed to work through, I gained a better understanding of my family, specifically my parents. I learned more about their lives and upbringing and how it dictated how they wanted to raise me and my brothers. I heard about their experiences moving to a country where they did not know the language and about how they went to places where they quickly realized they were not welcomed. I had always loved and respected my parents, but as I heard more about their lives, it made me so proud. I saw how resilient they were and how it caused me to be resilient too. I had so many low points in my life, but I was able to work my way through it. I was proud of the person I was becoming: a strong Hispanic woman.

Despite the way my college career started, I ended up graduating a semester early and immediately joined the workforce at an inpatient psychiatric hospital. Many of my undergrad classes revolved around mental health and substance misuse, so I was fortunate to get a job in the field I wanted. I knew that when I started the social work program, I wanted to be a Licensed Clinical Social Worker. I wanted to achieve the highest level of credentialing to show myself, and everyone else, that I could do it. I began applying to accredited master's programs and started looking at how I wanted to shape the next part of my education.

I was accepted into both master's programs I applied to. It was a hard choice, but I ultimately chose New York University. I felt like I had no real school spirit at community college, or at my university, and I wanted to change that for my master's program. I promised myself that I would be involved in my school as much as possible. During my two years there, I joined student government, took on a paid summer internship, and graduated with people who I believe will be lifelong friends. I felt so happy and learned so much, all while moving out of my parents' house and living on my own for the very first time.

I started my official career by working in foster care. It was not the field I planned to be in, as all my classes were regarding mental health, but I did not want to leave New York City. I thought it would be a place where I would stay for a few months until I got a "better" job. Within a few weeks, I absolutely fell in love with my agency. I was learning so many different things, felt incredibly supported, and like I was doing meaningful work. I felt fortunate that I got a job I looked forward to every day, and that I had a supervisor who was genuinely happy in helping me pursue my clinical license.

WISER, BUT STILL LEARNING

After I got my clinical license, I became a full-time supervisor and learned even more about myself and how others see me. At this time, the COVID-19 pandemic hit, and I felt the need to do more with my social work license. I opened up my own private practice, and try to ensure I make myself accessible to anyone interested in bettering their mental health. I also decided to change fields and left foster care to be part of an Intensive Mobile Treatment team. I was happy to be directly working in the mental health field again.

When I started my job after grad school, and even now, I see how policies have racial roots. Certain systems are stacked against people of color and systems are inherently keeping people down. I have become bolder in stating who I am and what I stand for. I have found friends and a husband who also see these injustices and want to do something about them. I have joined different organizations in hopes of creating meaningful and systemic change.

I am the first person on my mother's side to go to college and get a master's degree. I started my own private practice, and sometimes get paid to do photography. The sky is not the limit on what I can do, and I am so excited to see what the future holds. My younger self never envisioned that this would be my life. I am a Hispanic woman, and I am so proud.

REFLECTION

Why is social work so important today? Social work will always be important as long as there are oppressed, marginalized, and vulnerable communities and individuals. Social workers play a vital role in giving a voice to those whose voices are not being heard or properly understood. I feel that our profession is unique in that we don't have to fully understand a person's hardships to be an advocate for them.

Ask yourself, what gives you a purpose? And how has your purpose been shaped by your identity? Your purpose can also change over time, so don't resist the change, embrace it!

Also, don't be afraid of social media! Find individuals who have a similar mindset to yours. Join a network/committee for whatever your profession is. The National Association of Social Workers–NYC Chapter was an integral part of growing my network and gaining more insight about myself as a clinician. The Latino Social Work Coalition & Scholarship Fund has also provided me with so many different opportunities and resources during and after grad school.

ABOUT THE AUTHOR

Tania Vargas, LCSW is New York City-based but Florida-raised. Tania moved from her hometown of Tallahassee, Florida to pursue her master's in social work at New York University. Tania is an LCSW in the states of New York and New Jersey. She has worked in the child welfare system for New York City and has a passion for ending the stigma of having a mental health diagnosis.

Tania recently started her own private practice, Just A Little Step, LLC, in January 2021. She sees individuals, couples, and families through telehealth services. Along with owning her own private practice and being a supervisor, Tania is a photographer and consultant. Tania has been certified in four different curriculums regarding foster care and LGBTQ youth in the New York City foster care system. Thanks to ever-growing technology, you can reach Tania in multiple ways! Tania is always excited to talk to new people.

Tania Vargas
tania@justalittlestep.com
Instagram: taniavphotos
347-377-2380

RE-ESTABLISHING THE ROOTS OF COMMUNITY

DR. JASMIN COLLAZO, DSW, LCSW

To the outside world, the city I was born and raised in was often known as one of the "Top 25 Most Dangerous Cities in America." To me, it was not only home, but it was also my habitat—a natural place for me to achieve and grow. Yes, I saw the crime, but Newark, New Jersey was where my parents met, where I gained an extended family through my church, where everything I needed could be found downtown, and where my career for social work was launched.

I lived in the North section of Newark where the neighborhood blocks were predominantly filled with Latinos. This meant summers where the man selling piraguas rang his bell as he passed our neighborhood, where our local Puerto Rican parade was held every September, and the *empanadas* at the bodega were the best after-school snack.

Besides the obligatory family trips to Puerto Rico to visit extended family members, I never traveled outside of the tri-state area before I turned eighteen. Both my parents worked long and hard, and if I had my community of friends at church and my neighborhood, I was pretty much satisfied. I was always surrounded by Latinos and Blacks, which meant that the only thing I had to do to assert my Latina identity was say "I am Puerto Rican." I did not have to further explain my culture or heritage. I never felt like an outsider or an "other," and I was never made to feel like I was less than my peers.

UNDERGRADUATE SCHOOL

A few days after my eighteenth birthday, I was off to freshman orientation at Seton Hall University in South Orange, New Jersey. Although the town of South Orange borders the city of Newark, I knew that I entered a different world. From one block to another, the streetlights and concrete jungle of Newark turned into residential neighborhoods with tall houses and freshly manicured lawns.

I quickly noticed the disparities between a community of color and a predominantly White community. For the next four years, I would be experiencing the predominantly White college institution located in this predominantly White town. Now that I was here, this strange feeling came upon me that I was not going to fit in. This was in stark contrast to the pride I felt in being the first one in my family to go to college and gain scholarships that allowed me to study at a private university.

This thought of not fitting in became pervasive throughout my freshman year, and lingered throughout my undergraduate career as I encountered more interactions that highlighted the disparities between people of color and Whites.

I remember entering my freshman English class filled with my White peers talking about classic books read in high school that I had never heard about. These classic books were highlighted as notable works of literature that reflected the stories of White individuals and were often written by White authors. This furthers the harm that can be done to students of color in predominantly White institutions by increasing the feelings that devalue our self-worth. The message conveyed to us is that our stories are not seen as important enough to be taught in universities and passed down to future generations.

I also began to hear racist and stereotypical remarks, a common one being "If you are White, do not go to the right." I quickly realized that it was the City of Newark that was to the right of the school. This overt macroaggression felt like a direct blow to me. They were talking about my home, my community, and a piece of my identity. The longer I spent my days in school studying and working, away from my community, the more I felt less than my peers and "othered."

I did not realize it then, but as I reflect and write this chapter, I understand how important community is for Latinos, especially first-generation Latino college students. As a college student transitions from their home community, we begin to search for that community within the college setting. Usually, college students will find this through student organizations, fraternities, and sororities. This should bring awareness to universities, their student affairs departments, and student governments to the importance of establishing affinity groups for students of color, but also the importance in sustaining them. First generation college students, especially those of color, have a more difficult time adjusting to college, and it is the responsibility of universities to devote more time to prioritizing affinity groups that will aid this population. For me, joining the Adelante Latino/a Student Organization at Seton Hall transformed and solidified the meaning of community for me. It replicated not only the feelings of community that I experienced growing up in Newark, but it also helped me reassert my Latino identity and heritage.

Adelante brought a little piece of home to the college campus. Adelante's events were always filled with Latin music, Latin foods, and conversations filled with Spanglish. These important cultural aspects were rarely found on our college campus, but Adelante ensured that not only our culture would be highlighted, but our voices would be highlighted as well. Through different programming, Adelante always provided opportunities for people to share their stories, identities, traditions, and families. I distinctly remember standing in front of many students at one event and discussing the pride I had in being from Newark. This also allowed me to inform and confront the comments that were being made about my city and bring to light the harm this can do to students from our neighboring community. I could have used this opportunity to call people out, but instead I wanted to call them in, bringing deeper sense of self-awareness into the room.

Being vulnerable and sharing my feelings in front of a large group was not easy. I worried about the reception and perception of my words, especially when naming the overt racism embedded within the comments made about my community. However, knowing that my peers and members of the Adelante community were there helped me find and utilize more of my voice. I was even amazed and surprised at the number of non-Latinos who supported me and were consistently involved in Adelante's community meetings. This example only further served as a testament to the sense of community that Adelante established.

CAREER IN SOCIAL WORK

These experiences also had implications for my personal and professional development as a social worker while I was pursuing my undergraduate degree. As I gained a community in a home away from home, this further solidified the importance of working within my original community to push change forward. I was drawn towards working with children, adolescents, and young adults. I knew many individuals of this population who also felt isolated, who were marginalized, and who were just trying to be better than what the outside world made them out to be.

By the time I graduated in 2012, I no longer experienced that sense of being "less than" or the "other," I gained an extended family, and I felt excited to continue my journey as a budding social worker.

I continued to enjoy working with adolescents and young adults, and I worked with this population in residential and community settings both in my graduate field placements and as a professional social worker. I also ensured that I was dedicating part of my work towards my community, and would achieve this by working as a part-time in-home therapist in Newark. During my work as a clinical social worker working with individuals and families of color, I continually saw the needs and gaps in services, specifically in trauma-informed care.

As I was providing trauma treatment for my clients, I noticed that there were recurring themes that centered around fear of law enforcement, especially with my clients who experienced or witnessed domestic violence. This was around the same time that the United States Department of Justice released the results of their investigation into the Newark Police Department, where it was discovered that police officers were engaging in harmful police practices. I saw that trauma-informed care brought real, personal, and transformative changes to my clients, and I questioned why other systems were not following suit with trauma-informed approaches. I brought these questions to my family and friends who were in law enforcement, and they mentioned challenges related to training and officer mental health that were being ignored within the department and larger community.

GRADUATE SCHOOL

This served as the foundation that solidified my interest in the DSW program at NYU. I wrote the personal statement for my application about the City of Newark and the challenges within policing. I mentioned the primary and secondary victimization that police officers caused, and included in my application how I wanted to use the DSW degree towards promoting change within policing.

I was going to be a doctor. I was immensely grateful to God for this opportunity but equally fearful. All those feelings that I felt as I entered my undergraduate degree program at Seton Hall came flooding back again. Was I going to fit in? I felt even lonelier than when I was an undergraduate because I did not have mentors, family, or friends who had ever gone through a doctoral program. I truly felt as if I was traversing a new, unexplored world without so much as a compass, map, or tour guide.

As I attended orientation, I realized I was one of fourteen students in my cohort—and I was the only one who primarily identified as Latino. I should have felt proud at that moment, but the feelings of loneliness only further intensified.

That first semester of my doctoral program was especially challenging. I was adjusting to the exorbitant number of weekly readings and learning how to write an academic paper, after so much time had passed since my master's program. My biggest adjustment, however, was gaining the confidence to believe that I too belonged in this program as much as the rest of my classmates. I began to wonder if I had earned my place there or whether I was just a part of some diversity quota. As I listened to my classmates and got to know them, I saw marked differences in race, socioeconomic status, education, and social experiences.

This is also when I first learned about the imposter phenomenon and the accompanying feelings of inadequacy and self-doubt. However, it is important to emphasize that sometimes we (people of color) learn about imposter phenomenon and think that our experiences are internal struggles. Instead, we ought to take a closer look and critically reflect on whether our experiences with imposter phenomenon are just disguises for experiences with racism and discrimination. I now understand that my "imposter feelings" were just me facing the historic marginalization and exclusion of people of color in academia that is still ever present in our college classrooms.

Another challenge to my adjustment in my doctoral program was that I did not know of any communities in which I could ground myself in as I did with Adelante in my freshman year of college. The intense course load of the program only further isolated me from the communities that I had previously rooted myself in, such as my family, friends, and my faith. Although I connected with some of my classmates and began to develop lasting friendships, I never felt that it was enough. Furthermore, the quarantine mandates and shutdowns from the COVID-19 pandemic only deepened feelings of loneliness and isolation. I had to find alternatives towards reconnecting with communities previously established and develop new ones.

CONCLUSION

Communities do not have to be physical spaces nor consist of verbal interactions. As we all have reimagined ways to reconnect with our communities via virtual platforms like video conferencing and social media, we have also had more time to reflect and think about the things and people we want to ground ourselves in. Towards the end of my doctoral program, I delved into reading more books about Puerto Rican history and grounded myself in a community of Puerto Rican pride. I read books that deepened my spiritual beliefs and grounded myself in the community of my faith. I became a social work field instructor for the first time to a social work intern who was a Latina, effectively becoming part of a community of social work mentors/educators. This continues to strengthen me in the field of social work.

This is also why other social work professionals, especially those of color, need this book. The field of social work continues to be dominated by White professional social workers, even though social service consumers are predominantly people of color. This can leave young professional social workers experiencing imposter phenomenon, doubting their abilities, and questioning their resilience.

I will never forget the moment I presented a workshop towards the end of my doctoral degree and was told by a Latina how much she enjoyed seeing another Latina become a doctor. It made me reminisce of how I too needed someone like that early in my career, further validating the importance of creating and sustaining community.

REFLECTION

Social work continues (and will continue to be) a vital field that will only grow as the challenges of this world become increasingly complex. However, as much as there are new social workers that enter the field every year, there are also social workers who exit the field due to burnout. Social workers work tirelessly, and due to our human nature, we often forget or neglect to ground ourselves in things or people that will sustain us in the field.

It is only recently that self-care became an ethical mandate in our Code of Ethics. I encourage the reader to take the time to reflect on the things that brought them joy, to rediscover passions that encouraged a sense of fulfillment, and to reconnect to the communities that provided a foundation for sustainment. Lastly, I encourage all Latino social work professionals to reach out to one another. You never know how much your presence brings a sense of community to others.

ABOUT THE AUTHOR

Dr. Jasmin Collazo is a Licensed Clinical Social Worker from Newark, New Jersey, serving in a variety of social work roles. Dr. Collazo is an adjunct professor at New York University and owns a part-time private practice in New Jersey. She has a master's degree in social work and a Doctorate degree in social welfare (DSW), both from from New York University (NYU).

Remaining in the field of trauma-informed care, Dr. Collazo aspires to continue to use her private practice to serve adolescents, young adults, and police officers to advocate for changes within policing that are informed by those in the community she works with.

LAUDY BURGOS, LCSW-R

Growing up, college was not something that I generally had conversations about with my family. It wasn't until I started high school that I began these discussions with my family and learned that this was in fact something they hoped I would pursue. My mother hadn't attended college and my father only attended one semester before dropping out to start working because he was starting a family. They did always instill a sense of desire for achievement, however, in spite of their limited resources.

MY FIRST WOUND

I was born in Manhattan, NY and raised in West Harlem. I attended a public high school in East Harlem, and in my sophomore year, I was asked by my guidance counselor to start thinking about the college application process. She explained the benefits of higher education and what I could do with a college degree. From then on, I actually started thinking about college. I looked up majors, universities, and scholarships.

Initially, I was quite overwhelmed, and had many questions about the structure and process. She had to explain the difference between undergraduate and graduate school. I sat there feeling defeated, looking at this white woman with fancy jewelry and perfectly styled hair, not recognizing her white privilege. She may not have realized the impact of her approach, and how small it made me feel. Her microagressions harmed me.

I still remember that way she gazed at me, as if she could not see me; almost like she was looking past me. She stared at me impatiently, almost as if she was thinking she had ten more students to see that week that were just like me. In her eyes, we were kids who were never going to make anything of our lives.

It was clear to me that she doubted my potential given that I knew so little about higher education. Yet I was resilient and started doing research on the whole process. In my junior year, NYU offered a program called "Project MUST" which offered mentoring and taught leadership skills. During one of the field trips to NYU, I fell in love with the campus and knew that that is where I wanted to spend my college years. When I went to my guidance counselor, she told me that I would never get into NYU and my heart sank.

A BAND-AID

My parents insisted that I apply to NYU and any other schools I wanted. They believed in me. They were not fully aware of the full pain I felt after being discouraged by my guidance counselor. But their love and dedication helped me deal with the pain and kept me moving forward. They were hard-working people with strong family values, deep rooted traditions, and great faith. I reflected on this juxtaposition—she was saying I could not do it, but my parents believed I could. How can one be stronger than the other?

In that moment though, I decided to accept that Band-Aid that my parents placed over that incredible wound, knowing that it was going to be opened and reopened over and over again because I was a Brown woman.

The application process was daunting, and I had to do it mostly by myself, but my mother was right by my side when I visited the campus to request that they take another look at my financial aid package, since I had not received enough aid. Two weeks later, the much-anticipated letter arrived giving me almost a full ride. Other acceptance letters arrived, some from ivy league schools, but my heart was set on NYU.

Before I started my freshman year, I knew I wanted to be a social worker. My parents were both immigrants; my father worked as a shipping clerk in a dress factory and eventually became a supervisor through hard work and perseverance. Early on I knew that my parents' hard work and sacrifices committed me to a life of service.

I got a glimpse of what helping others would be like when I helped my grandmother and many of our neighbors fill out food stamp and housing applications. The gratitude in their eyes felt so rewarding. Also, as a Latina growing up in the late eighties and nineties in Harlem, I saw many people in my community struggle with poverty, substance abuse, and gun violence. A few of my peers would not have the chance to make it to college because they were pregnant, had to work, or had died.

BROWN GIRL PEELS OFF HER BAND-AIDS

Once in college, I became keenly aware that I had not had the privileges that many of my peers had grown up with. The biggest challenge for me was not seeing people who looked like me. It was extremely intimidating being the only brown girl in almost every class.

Despite being one of the top students in my high school graduating class, my writing was not at the level of many of my peers. The first few months I would get papers back with discouraging comments about my grammar and I developed impostor syndrome. The shame I felt made me question whether I truly belonged. Fortunately, a very special mentor in my BSW program helped me overcome these obstacles by directing me to the writing center, pointing out my strengths, and most importantly believing in me. This mentor was my angel throughout my undergraduate education. To this day, she continues to encourage me.

I had moments when I thought I could be successful, but I also had moments of ambivalence. Yet I walked through the door that I opened for myself. Seeing my father work many hours of overtime and the proud look on his face when he wore his NYU dad shirt also helped me push through. My grandmother also believed in me and reminded me that Latinos are a resilient and proud; and that we know how to overcome adversity and make the best of any situation. My first week at NYU, I saw her sitting in Washington Square Park, and she told me she brought the security guards *un cafecito* (small cup of coffee) with a picture of me so they would look after me and keep me safe. It is this warmth and family connection within our Latino culture that helped me thrive. Shortly after, I walked through Washington Square Park with my purple sweater feeling confident and smart, and ready to thrive!

Within a year, I was writing like my peers and flourishing. I began peeling off these mental Band-Aids and realizing I was slowly healing through my own resilience. I was feeling brave enough to be successful.

I began interacting more with other students and got involved with activities. I also organized a toy drive that benefitted a Pediatric HIV program at NYU Hospital. This was my first glimpse into medical social work. After speaking to the social worker on the unit, I knew this was something I would definitely consider. Around this time, I became aware of all the obstacles my family faced when navigating the healthcare system. My mother always needed me to translate, which was not always appropriate, and my grandmother saw multiple primary care doctors who prescribed many medications for her chronic illnesses, not ever assessing what else she was taking.

In my junior year, my mentor and I were discussing these healthcare challenges and she encouraged me to intern at a hospital, so I could see if it was a good fit for me. I was placed in pediatric psychiatry, and a whole world of possibilities opened up for me. Not only did I learn excellent assessment and intervention skills, but I began to understand how illness (physical and mental) affects the individual and the family system. Again, I noticed that the majority of the patients treated in hospital mental health clinics were people of color with Medicaid. This meant long wait lists, different doctors, and having to switch doctors when their training ended. This lack of consistency creates disparities in care.

Graduating with a BSW from NYU is to date one of the best moments of my life. While I yearned to continue on to obtain my MSW, I began worrying about how to pay for it. Once again, my mentor encouraged me to apply to the MSW program, reminding me that all challenges are opportunities for growth. Once in the MSW program at NYU, she helped me get a job at an Early Head Start Program, and I was lucky enough to work with amazing social workers who invested in me and taught me. Before I knew it, I had graduated!

THE MANY PHASES OF SOCIAL WORK

As I sit here in the midst of a pandemic and I reflect, I recall my past twenty-three years in my social work career. I thought about what I have accomplished and also the work I still need to do. I am now a manager supervising an entire program area. As a woman in a leadership position, I think about how I used my power to effect change and to support others' healing. In the Summer of 2020 in response to the George Floyd murder, my colleague and I created safe virtual spaces for staff to express their rage, fear, outrage, and the need to dismantle racism within the institution. This led to us partnering with the Social Work Department leadership to create the Social Work Anti-Racism & Inclusion Initiative. Every place I have ever entered, I have wanted to dismantle racism, reduce health disparities, educate, support, and mentor. I am extremely grateful for my friend and colleague who has held me accountable in this work, while celebrating our accomplishments. I am also grateful for the leader working with us who has taken a leap of faith and not only helped us develop our vision, but engaged in difficult conversations with us to develop our initiatives in an intentional way. This too helps me heal that initial wound.

My first job out of graduate school was in Pediatric Asthma at a hospital. During my five and a half years there, I worked with the Centers for Disease Control, helping families overcome psychosocial stressors so that they could manage their child's asthma. I learned that East Harlem has one of the highest incidences of asthma in the country, and I felt honored to play a part in addressing this. Environmental factors, psychosocial stressors, and access to care were all issues that impacted my patients and their families. I wanted to do more, so I joined the Asthma Working Group, a community-based group that advocated for better living conditions for these families. I spoke with legislators and wrote grants that resulted in programs that benefitted my patients.

In 2004, I began working in OB/GYN-Women's Health at the same hospital. Working with poor, minority, pregnant women was very different, but I quickly realized many issues remained the same: health disparities, inadequate housing, mental illness, poverty, and more. All these issues impacted outcomes for their babies. As the teen social worker, I became very passionate about teaching my teen patients everything I could to prepare them for parenting to ensure better outcomes for themselves and their children. In this position, I was also fortunate to be supervised by a very wise mentor of color who shared her gifts generously in the form of mentorship. She taught me how to survive in spaces where systemic racism exists.

In 2012, I became interested in postpartum depression and how this affects an already vulnerable population of women of color. For almost ten years, I have received training to ensure that I can help as many women as possible, so that they can feel confident about parenting and explore their full potential. During my time here, I have also had the opportunity to publish my work, which has been incredibly rewarding professionally.

For the past fourteen years I have also worked as a consultant with various foster care agencies doing adoption home studies and working with youth to prepare them for adulthood. It has opened my eyes to the fact that despite many challenges that exist in the foster care system, there are many opportunities to intervene which will result in huge impacts to children's lives.

I have also had the privilege of teaching and advising students at NYU, Columbia University, and Fordham University. Sharing my knowledge and seeing students learn a particular concept is one of my favorite things in the world! They too have taught me so much about the values and ethics of social work.

However, the two things I am most proud of in my social work career are my role as a mentor and my work in anti-racism and inclusion. In the summer of 2019, I assumed leadership of the Northeast Regional Alliance (NERA) Behavioral Health Undergraduate Social Work Fellowship at my institution. This is a pipeline program that targets disadvantaged college juniors majoring in social work or psychology to impact awareness and preparation for competitive application to graduate school programs in social work. Many of the students are people of color like me, who overcame obstacles and made it to college. Many of them benefit from learning professional and social work skills that will take them to the next level in their professional careers. Seeing the fellows from my first cohort graduate with their MSW this past May was a proud moment for me.

Both are true examples of the roots of social work: social justice, activism, advocacy, and a moral obligation to help society's most vulnerable. To know that I am making a difference in the lives of people of color who struggle with racial trauma gives me immense satisfaction. The work is challenging because we know that systemic racism and oppression are difficult to dismantle, but the values in our Latino culture have carried me through: family, the importance of human connection, compassion, and perseverance.

Being a Latina means having to work extra hard to prove your worth in this country, but my passion has seen me through many obstacles. I thank my husband and children who inspire me daily. They look up to me and celebrate all my accomplishments. They remind me that I serve as a role model to them, and I see myself in them in the way they walk through their journey.

My deepest love and gratitude to my parents and sisters who always believed in me and put all those Band-Aids, so that I could push through. Their support got me through many nights while I studied and wrote papers.

REFLECTION

Today, social workers go beyond providing support to people and connect them to resources to actively address the problems that prevent societal change and progress. It moves beyond service to social reform. Through our work we can bring awareness to issues among marginalized communities. Our field is evolving and there are opportunities to engage in more political work that will impact change from micro to macro levels. Our role is holistic and can be far-reaching.

- Why is it important to address how race impacts disparities in health?
- Why is it important to understand racial trauma when working with BIPOC?
- Why is it important to discuss white privilege and have uncomfortable conversations?
- Why is it important to develop mentorship programs for social work students?
- Why is it important to work with a variety of populations?
- What parts of your Latino culture do you bring into your work?
- How can you become an effective agent of change?

ABOUT THE AUTHOR

Laudy Burgos, LCSW is a social work manager in the Women's and Children's Division at Mount Sinai Hospital. In this capacity, she supervises social work staff in the outpatient clinic, inpatient units, and the faculty practice in the OB/GYN Department. Her specialty area is the treatment of perinatal mood disorders. She is also a New York co-coordinator for Postpartum Support International and is a board member for The Perinatal Mental Health of Alliance for People of Color.

She has presented at various national and international social work conferences and is the author of "Screening for Perinatal Depression in an Inner-City Prenatal Setting" and co-author of "Postpartum mood among universally screened high and low socioeconomic status patients during COVID 19 social restrictions in New York City" and "Early pregnancy mood before and during COVID-19 community restrictions among women of low socioeconomic status in New York City: a preliminary study." She also works as a consultant for several foster care agencies in New York City.

Laudy is currently on faculty at the Icahn School of Medicine at Mount Sinai, Columbia University School of Social Work, and NYU Silver School of Social Work. She is a graduate of the New York University Silver School of Social Work.

Madrina

MAKING A SOCIAL WORKER: A TRIBUTE TO TRANSFORMATIONAL LEADERSHIP

MARIA ELENA GIRONE, MSW

"Never cease in making your dreams your reality."

THE JOURNEY BEGINS: THE ONSET OF COMPASSION AND EMPATHY

I grew up in the small mountain town of Ciales, Puerto Rico. Life was very simple, and the main institutions that gave life to the community were the Catholic Church, a tobacco factory, and storefronts carrying essentials. Two drugstores supplied medical equipment and other necessities; no banks or financial institutions were available at the time.

The local economy was mostly dependent on coffee crops, tobacco, and sugar cane. A small hospital provided outpatient care, and there were only two doctors to meet non-urgent medical needs. This fragile health infrastructure was backed only by the larger hospitals located in the larger nearby municipalities. Gravely ill patients often died before reaching the district hospital, which was two to three hours away by car.

In these less-than-ideal circumstances, there was complete absence of mental health care. Those in need of specialized mental health services were locked up in a small cement building with pigeon hole openings that simulated windows. I remember going close to the building with a group of children my age in youthful curiosity, and listening to the yelling and the attempts of some patients to climb the walls just to have a narrow glimpse of the sun. These experiences led me to believe that people suffering from mental illness were dangerous and in need of custodial care.

My earliest role models in successful, compassionate, and people-centered leadership were my parents and the church. The Catholic Church was the primary faith-based institution in our town—as such, the local priest (Father Beltran) was an authority figure towards whom people gravitated. My father, with his knowledge of "Cooperativas" (gathering together of investors), was the perfect ally for our priest, and they worked together for the benefit of our community; they devoted themselves to the task of creating Ciales' first financial organization—the "Cooperativa Catolica de Ciales." To this day, the organization is a vibrant force in the community, driving much of the financial prosperity of Ciales.

This partnership was my earliest education in two of the most important elements of nonprofit leadership: strategic planning and funding. Ciales needed a new church—Father

Beltran and my father were up to the challenge of making it happen. From getting the backing of the Cooperativa, to mobilizing the community to support via fundraising and in-kind contributions, the dream was finally realized.

Today, that church still stands as an architectural testament to the outstanding history of leaders working together for the wellbeing of the community. I didn't know it then, but the same way that my father worked to make sure the building blocks for that church were laid down, his leadership and example laid the building blocks for my own future as social worker and a leader.

THE VALUE OF AN EDUCATION FROM UNLIKELY PLACES

I am a firm believer that early life experiences give shape to our character and our success in the future. My father was the only bookkeeper in the local tobacco factory; he was also very keen on teaching me the ins and outs of keeping a ledger. My deep interest in completing my education and getting as many tools under my belt as possible comes from my parents' unconditional support and investment in my future. This early exposure to finances was incredibly valuable in the future, when I became involved in the development and purchase of property for the housing of PRFI programs. The initiation and completion of capital projects were immensely important parts of my tenure as president and CEO of that grand organization.

Another early experience that crystallized for me the importance of compassion in this work and had a profund influence in my later career choices was witnessing early on the way that those less fortunate had to navigate the world. It was a common occurrence in my town for a local sex worker to have encounters with the police. She was a mother of five children, who was often placed under arrest, and since the precinct was not far from where I lived, they often had to pass by my house on their way to the police station. I still remember hearing her children crying in the night, as they trailed their mother, walking in front of them in handcuffs towards the detention center. I was only ten, but I felt deeply the suffering of those children, and witnessing their pain left me with a profound sense of right and wrong. This memory inspired in me a desire to explore a career path that would enable me to alleviate the suffering of children. Little did I know then, that this desire would lead me to a career in social work.

BAPTISM BY FIRE: READY OR NOT, YOU'RE IN CHARGE

I was a driven student, and finished my bachelor's degree early, entering the job market with all the energy and excitement that only youth can bring. I was fortunate enough to find a social work-related position after graduation, and was hired to manage a welfare center (that's what they were called back then!) in my town, overseeing its child welfare services and public assistance program.

My first challenge was earning the respect of my colleagues and staff. This can be hard to do when you're younger than they are, and have the youthful appearance to match. From the custodian all the way to the senior staff, they insisted on referring to me as "nena," a term of endearment, which frustrated me to no end. But I realized that their respect had to be earned, a task which I set to diligently accomplish in those early days. The opportunity would present itself in no time.

One of my duties a manager was to assist the staff in interventions with clients with children, by connecting them to programming that would help them develop a sense of ownership over their lives. One of our center's clients was none other than the aforementioned sex worker from my town (I'll call her Client X). This woman was still engaged in sex work, and over the years, her interactions with law enforcement and other agencies led her to mentally deteriorate and act out. Her behaviors only escalated, leading to violent episodes and recurring threats and intimidation against authority figures. One day, she came into the office with a knife, ready to cut the face of her public assistance worker, who had closed her case due to noncompliance. I remember the dread of realizing that I had to step in; I was in charge. Even though I was afraid for my own life, I needed to protect by team (and our client, who was in our care).

This was my first lesson in administration and client center management: always have a plan! I quickly jumped to action, and diffused the situation by engaging Client X in a conversation (heated at first, then calmer) about how she would find in me a sympathetic ear, as long as her interactions with staff were based on respect and non-violence.

Shortly after that, I was offered the opportunity to obtain my master's degree. I went on to earn my social work degree from the University of Puerto Rico, Rio Piedras. My early experiences as a manager solidified in me the realization that I had what it takes to confront difficult challenges, to lead teams successfully, and to find joy and satisfaction in a job well done. This experience and knowledge were imprinted in me throughout my social work education/career: even if you are intimidated or afraid, the people under our care rely on us to be brave, be strong, and to lead confidently (regardless of our age).

FINDING A PURPOSE AND COMMUNITY IN THE BIG APPLE

I did not intend to stay in New York. My first impression was it was a gloomy city made of steel and bricks, a radical contrast with sunny Puerto Rico. I missed the warm weather of the island and the warmth of its people, always ready with a smile and friendly welcome of "Familia!" whether they knew you or not.

This greeting, while not yet fashionable, was prevalent in Latino communities, and was a reassuring comfort I found in my close-knit network of aunts and cousins in New York. They asked for me to stay. I, never one to back down from a new challenge or exciting experience, decided to do so.

The feeling of being a stranger in a strange land is an uneasy one to navigate, and for Puerto Ricans in particular, with our complex political status within the mainland, it can be a challenging landscape. In those early days of my living in

New York City, ethnic divisions, rampant violence, and brutal personal attacks became part of my day-to-day experience. The language barrier was also a source of discomfort and unease. Even though English as a second language was a standard part of the curriculum in Puerto Rico, conversational English was a major challenge of city life here in the States.

My discovery of the Puerto Rican Family Institute led to an instant love for its mission and purpose. The focus on strengthening families and providing much needed support in the transition to city life for Puerto Rican migrants as well as Latino immigrants was deeply alluring to me, as this was also my experience. I joined a staff of four social workers, and quickly learned how deeply we felt the calling to assist our community in making a successful transition to a foreign country with different cultural expectations, a different language, and varying ways of life. I found a community of leaders whose talents were well suited in pushing the Institute's mission forward.

The importance of smart board composition was a valuable lesson from those early days. The non-social workers at the Institute were reflective of the community that we served, and were devoted to the mission of driving the organization forward; we acquired board members that were highly interested in and had the potential to contribute to the success of our programs and our clients.

The Institute became my professional "nest," meeting my deep desire to serve my people and to open pathways for them to work against the undermining factors so prevalent in communities of color; lack of culturally and linguistically competent service; the marginalization that comes from having access to resources; and the blights of interpersonal violence, mental illness, and poverty. At the time, we were running with an experimental budget of $250K, funded under an anti-poverty initiative. Often, money was unavailable for salaries. But the devotion and persistence of our small band of Puerto Rican social workers was unrelenting.

With all the vigor and potency that goes into starting a movement, I was introduced to a new world order of public demonstrations to elevate in the public discourse the plight of Latinos, and how we could alleviate those challenges. To this day, the inroads made by my contemporaries, pioneers who bravely spoke out against injustices to our community, set the stage for the organizations that became integral parts of the fabric of Latino-based helping institutions in New York. Many of those Puerto Rican leaders are responsible for the changes in public policy and organizations driving those changes: ASPIRA, PRACA, and the Institute for Hispanic Elderly come to mind.

I became part of the formation of the Coalition of Hispanic Family and Children's Services, together with the extraordinary leadership of Jose Nazario (who later went on to be one of the Latino Social Work Coalition's co-founders).

Many of my fellow Puerto Ricans were involved in the expansion of the Hispanic Counseling Center, and I was a member of the group that established the Hispanic Federation. ACACIA NETWORK has been a source of pride for our community, with their ever-expanding reach and ability to provide mentorship and guidance to our emerging Latino leaders interested in creating and supporting our own institutions. Organizations and leaders such as these were paramount in the development of programs and services to serve our communities. Some of the most important facets of these programs focused on included breaking intergenerational cycles of dependency, strengthening families by keeping them together, influencing public policy, and alleviating the effects of poverty. Important to this process was the understanding that moving forward TOGETHER is the wisest way to proceed for our organizations and our communities.

REFLECTION

1. What is your dream? Dare to dream regardless of how small or big.
2. Do you struggle asking for help? You are not alone; if you ask you will receive.
3. Keep those in power accountable, it is our God-given duty.

ABOUT THE AUTHOR

Maria Girone has dedicated 50 years of her professional life to realize the above stated mission. She obtained her academic degrees from the University of Puerto Rico, with a bachelor's degree in political science and a master's degree in social work. Prior to her master's program, she worked as a director of a public welfare office in her hometown in Puerto Rico, managing its public assistance and child welfare programs.

In 1965, she relocated to New York City, where she joined The Puerto Rican Family Institute, a very small, developing nonprofit. The Institute provided the perfect platform for the initiation and realization of her vision. Her entire career was therefore closely linked to the development of the Institute, which under her leadership became a premier, culturally competent human and health family-oriented organization. In 1982, she became regional director, and in 1986, president and CEO.

Still cognizant of her vision to create Latino based institutions, she established the Hope for Families Foundation in 1989, which aimed to become a fund development supportive organization for the Institute, thus providing a vehicle for financial stability and capital investments.

All in all, the Institute enjoyed tremendous expansion, and prosperity during her tenure. She retired at the end of 2014, leaving at her departure two solid financially strong organizations with a financial base in excess of $100 million, between capital and grants.

Investing in her profession has been a cause very close to her heart. Therefore in 2001, with the able partnership of the Social Work Association New York City Chapter the present Latino Social Work Coalition and Scholarship Fund Inc was founded. In addition to the founding partners, several schools of social work and other nonprofits gave themselves the task to address the shortage of culturally competent Latino social workers in New York Social and Health systems of care. The Coalition has become a major provider of scholarships funds, thus increasing the number of social work graduates mainstreaming in our service systems.

Madrina

SOCIAL WORKERS CHANGED MY LIFE

MARIA LIZARDO, LMSW

"Always find the time to find your joy."

The reason I chose to be a social worker is tied to my childhood and my upbringing. I was born in the United States, in New York City. My parents came here from the Dominican Republic in 1965, to escape political unrest and extreme poverty. My mom was the youngest of sixteen kids, illiterate, and only completed a third-grade education. My dad was the oldest of two, and had his high school diploma.

They came here when there were few Dominican Latinos in New York City. They settled in the Hamilton Heights, Washington Heights, area because it was cheaper, and that's where they decided to begin living their American dream. My father worked in a steak restaurant and was an abusive gambler. My mom worked in factories.

When I was four and my sister was two, we were shipped off to the Dominican Republic, because they were going to start saving for a house there. We lived there for four years, and that is where I started my formal education. That is the reason I am Spanish dominant.

We returned to New York City when I was eight, because my mom realized that my dad had gambled away all the money that they had been saving. She decided it was time to bring her kids back home so she could raise them. Then she had my brother, and when I turned sixteen, it was me, my sister, who is two years younger, my brother, and my mom. My older sister, from a previous relationship, was living in the D.R. at that time with her husband.

Moving back to the U.S. was harsh, not only because we went from a tropical climate to the cold, but the pace is busier here—and I only knew Spanish. I also was in a higher grade there, and here they put me in the third grade.

I was so grateful for our Cuban neighbors, and the girl in their family, Tamara, became my best friend and helped to teach me English. There were no bilingual classes at that time.

PROJECT BASEMENT

We lived down the block from a community-based organization called Project Basement. That's the place where the social workers impacted and changed the course of our lives. They connected us to the free school breakfast and lunch programs, they filled out my first summer youth application at the age of fourteen, and I worked at a camp in Harlem as a tutor.

That's when I decided to become a social worker, because it was those three social workers, Susan, Kathy and Annie, at Project Basement that had such a great influence on our whole family. They hired me the next year to work at their after-school programming, and then I stayed with them. I worked after school, went to high school, and then when I finished high school, they hired me full time.

I was a case manager in the preventive program. Then, at the age of twenty-three, I graduated from Hunter College, and a few years later, decided to go to graduate school at Hunter College School of Social Work.

It was that nonprofit, and those women who showed us that they cared, that wove themselves throughout our lives and had such a profound impact. It was that community that saw the potential that we had, and believed that we could all do better. They gave us hope because we grew up poor. There were times when we didn't have money for meat, and we had white rice and scrambled eggs, because that's all there was. To this day, it's one of my favorite meals.

My mom was also a huge influence. She was fierce, a *guerrera*, a warrior who came to New York for a better life. There were four things that she taught us—education is key, you must work hard, you have to make space for yourself at the table because no one is going to do it for you, and you have to be of service to others. It's not enough that you do for yourself; you must take care of your neighbors and your community.

FINDING MY PASSION

After I graduated from college with my bachelor's degree in sociology, I got a job at PROMESA in the Bronx, and I was with them for eight years, full-time. I did a variety of different things there. I worked with the runaways and homeless youth, substance abusers, ambulatory methadone, and residential drug-free clients.

Then they started a community development unit, and I moved over to that. When I made that switch, I became more embedded in community work. And that's where I found my passion. That's what I really enjoyed, working with developing youth councils and neighborhood councils.

I was also doing tenant organizing, supervising buildings, and program development. That's where I became passionate about doing those program pieces. And my supervisor, Cindy Coulter, was another person who really influenced me. That's when I decided to go to social work school, and the organization was supportive of letting me go.

It was a one-year residency program with one full day of classes and four days of an internship at PROMESA. When I graduated with my master's in social work from Hunter College with a major in community organizing, I went to work at NMIC, who I found through my fellow organizer back in those days, as there was no internet.

WORKING FOR NMIC=FULFILLED

In June 1998, I started at NMIC as the director of social services. I've been there ever since. As it turned out, I was promoted to assistant executive director, in February 2014, became the interim executive director, and then in November 2014, I was appointed executive director. I didn't come to NMIC thinking I was going to stay there for twenty-three years, but it has been a great opportunity for me to work in my community, to work with many Dominicans, and to really give back to the community that raised me and supported me throughout my childhood.

The diversity of the programming work that I was doing in the community, building those connections and relationships, has kept me fulfilled. I think because the makeup is so diverse in the programming that we do, I'm always learning and growing. That's important to me, because I don't like to be bored or stagnated. Seeing the impact that we have on the Dominican community is also important to me—I am able to give back to my people, who are still the majority of the residents in Washington Heights and the Bronx neighborhoods we serve.

MACRO SOCIAL WORKER

As a macro social worker, I have the skills to work in all areas, from ACS to working with individuals, doing therapy, group work, or macrowork, where we are looking to move the needle when it comes to the city and communities.

Even more, I look at that work: how do we impact the policies that affect our communities? How do we make those big changes that have a larger impact on more folks? I did community organizing because it's important for folks to understand and know their rights, to know that they have what it takes to bring about changes. Whether it is changes in their buildings or in the community, the city, whatever it is, they have that power.

I want to do the kind of work that impacts a lot of people, and that includes policy. That also includes budgets, because a budget is a moral document, and when you don't have your elected officials or your government investing in communities, then we must be the collective that pushes them to change how they allocate resources.

That is a big part of my job—to hold elected officials accountable for the promises they made to their community members and constituents. How do I hold them accountable? How do I make sure that I leverage the resources that they have available to them and bring that back into the community? I do that by building good working relationships with them. I also do it by being adversarial when I have to be—calling them out, whether that is to their face, on letters, or on social media.

THE BRIDES MARCH

We started our domestic violence project because of three women who had been murdered in the neighborhood. So, we started a program because we recognized that domestic violence was an issue in our community, and there weren't many non-residential programs to support survivors in their own communities.

Then, on September 26th, 1999, Gladys Ricart was murdered by her abusive ex-boyfriend on the day of her wedding, in her New Jersey home, in front of her family and friends as she was taking pictures. It was devastating because it was an act of violence, but it also divided the community, with some folks saying she deserved it, and advocates saying she was a victim and no one deserves to be murdered.

At that point, we held a community vigil. We gathered with other domestic violence providers, and we went to the funeral because we were so moved by what had happened to her. We went on about our work supporting survivors until 2001, when Josie Ashton, from Florida, reached out to the Violence Intervention Program. She wanted to do a march from Gladys' home all the way down to Miami, Florida, in her wedding gown, in order to raise awareness, and along the way, she would stay at different domestic violence shelters.

The Ricart family gave their blessing, and the first Brides March took place on September 26th, 2001. The March was organized by Josie Ashton, the Ricart family, Dominican Women's Development Center (DWDC), Northern Manhattan Improvement Corporation (NMIC), the National Dominican Women's Caucus, the National Latino Alliance for the Elimination of Domestic Violence, and the Violence Intervention Program (VIP).

We started at Gladys' house in Ridgefield, New Jersey, and walked that entire day, all the way to Flushing, Queens, where she was going to get married the day of her murder. For us, it was important to do what Gladys would have done that day. That was the same time her murderer was on trial.

It was supposed to be a one-day event, but this year the 21st Brides March was held in September. We started in Washington Heights, marched into the Bronx, and we ended in East Harlem, because these are still communities that are highly impacted by domestic violence. And we want to make sure that survivors know they're not alone.

The march has grown from a handful of folks the first year to several hundred people, and has become a movement with marches in other areas—the Dominican Republic, Rhode Island, Florida, Yonkers, and Washington D.C. Even my son has been involved since he was little, and continues to participate today. It's definitely a way to continue to raise awareness and to remember Gladys, and with participants wearing wedding gowns, it catches people's attention.

WE ARE CHANGE AGENTS

The work that I do is based on the fact that I know social workers do have an impact. I know that social workers can impact individuals, can impact families, and we can also impact communities.

We are those change agents. For me, this is not just about work. I'm invested in this because I have lived it. I have experienced the impact that we have. I know I would not be in the role I'm in today or be able to do the things that I'm doing if it were not for those social workers.

I think, for social workers, it's really about finding what brings you joy and then making sure that you do them, because otherwise, you will burn out. I tell every young social worker or new social worker, try different things in the profession until you find what you're passionate about, because even when you get tired, it is that passion that you come back to. It's what keeps you energized and in the profession.

For those new to social work, you need to build your network of people who support you, but you also need to have those more seasoned professionals who can share their experiences with you, and that helps to guide you as well. I always tell young social workers that you have a responsibility as you grow in this field to give back, because it is about giving back and lifting other social workers while you are on your journey.

REFLECTION

The COVID-19 pandemic has demonstrated the important role the social work profession has in supporting communities. In the midst of a worldwide pandemic, social workers have shown up for communities in ways that most people now recognize as "essential." As we look toward the future, social workers will be key in planning and implementing strategies that will move communities from merely surviving to communities that are thriving.

As a profession, we have a responsibility to not only focus on the micro work that is impacting individuals, but also on the macro work that will change systems, thereby impacting communities at large. I am a proud social worker. I am proud to be part of a profession that looks at the world from a strength-based perspective and proud to be part of a profession that supports and builds on the resiliency of its people and communities. I can't say it enough. I am a proud social worker.

REFLECTION

1. What brings you joy?
2. What helps you refill your tank?
3. What keeps you grounded in your work?

ABOUT THE AUTHOR

Maria Lizardo is a proud Dominican-American who serves her community as executive director of Northern Manhattan Improvement Corporation (NMIC), leading a team of nearly 150 attorneys, educators, social workers, counselors, organizers, advocates, and volunteers. Under her leadership, NMIC serves over 14,000 low-income immigrant community members each year, with programs to address their housing, immigration, benefits/finance, health, education/career, and holistic needs.

Her passion and talent for organizing broadens her impact; she is a leading advocate in our community, and ensures our collective voice extends to the city, state, and national level. For example, she is a founding driver of the Brides' March to address domestic violence in the Latinx community, which has been a local rallying point for two decades, and expanded as far as Florida and the Dominican Republic.

Maria has been service-oriented her entire life, having worked at PROMESA, Inc. before joining NMIC in 1998, where she implemented numerous tenant, youth, open space, and safety programs. She earned her master of social work degree from the Silberman School of Social Work at Hunter College, and pairs her education with her lived experiences as a Hamilton Heights and Washington Heights native. She serves as a catalyst for positive change in the lives of our immigrant community members.

Maria Lizardo
lizardo823@gmail.com
IG: @marializardo702
917-940-0384

FROM PRECARITY TO PURPOSE

AMELIA ORTEGA, LCSW

ROOTS

I learned early in my life about precarity. The precarity of presence, of selfhood, of money, future, anger, emotions, and of being witnessed. Social work interestingly, is a field that carries a long history of being a work that operates at the edges of precarity. It is a field that asks us to move toward the places in ourselves that reflect that precarity of life, the delicate and violent ways that systems define us, and oppression that binds us. I learned early in my life that to be seen is to take a risk, to step into the precarious nature of another's emotions, and the volatility of possibility for conflict.

I grew up in a small town in Southern Rhode Island, a child of a Mexican immigrant and a white mother. The 1980s shaped my story deeply—as I was one of the only multiracial children I knew, my brother and I were often the only Latinx kids in our classes.

My father, a Vietnam Veteran, understood precarity—some of what he understood was passed to me before I was old enough to pass it back. His life as a union carpenter was a life in the summer sun, and winter cold, building homes and pouring concrete for businesses. My mother, a fiber artist, finished a vocational high school to become a typist in the 1960s and to find a life outside the multi-generational traumas of alcoholism her family gifted her. To share a narrative about my path to social work, I must include an acknowledgement of their paths too. So much of my understanding of myself, of my healing work, of my career trajectory has held a reflection of each of them.

As a working class, multiracial family in New England, collectively we knew a lot about precarity—both the heart-racing effects of a layoff and the excitement of a Union Book full of stamps for a trade in at the holidays.

As an artist, my mother gave me my first examples of mutual aid and anti-capitalism in action. I would often see her being given rides from AlAnon meetings by fellow members, passing patterns and designs through her community of weavers, and bartering weaving lessons for pastries with our local bakery owner.

My path to social work has been shaped by the values of community care and the power of collective labor that were passed to me through the experiences of my Mexican family immigrating to the U.S. in the 1950s (a grueling decade of assimilation and white supremacy) and my mother's creative approaches to meeting her needs in healing. Both parts of my lineage carry stories of literally building from the places that are most uncertain, and skills for navigating precarity in literal war and daily life. These skills are deeply ingrained in my own story and the narrative of my path toward social work.

QUEERNESS AS A PATH

At fifteen, I came out to my family and a few friends as queer. It was 1995, I lived in a racially ambiguous body, I lived in a small town, and I was living through the initial years when state legislations were passing bills to acknowledge and protect LGBTQ youth. I came out on the heels of the AIDS epidemic and during a powerful time when federal money from the Ryan White CARE Act was trickling through the Eastern States to fund LGBTQ youth programs. I joined Rhode Island's only LGBTQ youth organization and found a whole world waiting for me.

Three days a week, I would leave high school and take a one and a half-hour bus ride to Providence, completing my homework on the ride. I'd make it just in time for support groups, snacks, flirting, and, most importantly, meeting with a counselor.

I met my first social worker at age sixteen. She was a queer adult who offered time, acknowledgement, resources, and a path forward. Sessions were a resting place for me, and they also served as a fiery, generative space for inner turmoil and sadness to be released.

The harassment I was facing from peers, select teachers, and my principal left me isolated and hypervigilant. Through my social worker, I was networked with other queer youth experiencing homophobia in their high schools. I became a youth speaker, advocate, and organizer, and in 1997, I founded the second Gay Straight Alliance in my state—and I learned again the power that comes from collective action. I was provided Pro Bono legal services through GLAAD (Gay & Lesbian Advocates and Defenders) to take on the principal denying my Gay Straight Alliance school funding—and we won.

The support of my social worker, her guidance, and belief in me gave me a perspective on my future. It honored my anger and germinated the beginning of my career dedicated to supporting LGBTQ community.

As a Latinx queer youth, I found my place with other Latinx young people through Youth Pride Inc. I wasn't asked to choose queerness or racial identities. I was held in this community that accepted the wholeness of young people. These years of early organizing and community building gave me a new name for myself: social change maker.

Like many social workers, I came to this work because of the modeling of my own social worker. When faced with the question of attending college, my social worker told me about the alternative college she attended, and I applied and eventually graduated from there as well. The clear link to the future this adult gave me is a critical component of our work as social work providers.

I found my way to an MSW program after many years of volunteering and work as a young adult working in LGBTQ youth programs and queer youth organizing spaces. This work is complicated, and I consider these moments of modeling in my own career the gemstones that shine through the trauma of this work.

RADICAL MOVEMENTS AS A MEANS OF SURVIVAL

Examining my path to social work, it is easy to identify the years when the work itself brought up critically important questions about ethics, the role of state control in our profession and the difficulty of social change under racial capitalism. Community organizing and critical care work for LGBTQ BIPOC communities often exists at the margins of mainstream social services. Queer BIPOC communities have survived for generations due to intricate networks of mutual aid, intergenerational wisdom transmission, and art practices. We are a brilliant and creative people. We are a network, a web, a series of chosen families, a movement for living despite the persistence of oppression and death—and social workers have not always understood. Social workers have historically been complicit within systems of power and oppressive state sanctioned violence. This is especially true when examining Queer histories.

There is great power in the title of social worker, and for many years after graduate school, I actually didn't wish to identify with the title. Case manager, community support worker, group leader, and harm reduction worker all summed up the work more accurately than "social worker." It is now that I claim this title, with a new clarity about my capacity to influence our field.

Social work carries a complex history of savior syndrome, white supremacy, complicit behavior in anti-blackness and the policing of families, and the upholding of classist values against low-income communities. It is hard not to see these histories alive in all the titling and language that accompany the field. This language is present in the national MSW curriculum, standards of ASWB and the gatekeeping held in the licensing process.

The history of white supremacy is a present-day history—and denial of this is the single largest problem facing our profession's ability to grow and to meet the needs of BIPOC providers who are on the path to licensing. To really own the title of social worker means to acknowledge and own the legacies it holds and to locate yourself within this larger story.

As a Latinx social worker, I am dedicated to naming the structures of harm that our profession has been silent about for many generations. This silence has prevented other Latinx folks from feeling that their experience in social work education and the field are seen and valid.

A key to the navigation of my career path has been the mentoring and support from other Latinx and queer-identified providers. I graduated from my MSW program with a network of fellow Latinx students, and we built this network through our Latinx student organization. However, it became quickly apparent that we needed to know folks who were further along in their careers, and who were also interested in opening doors.

I did not find that all senior level social workers were interested in opening doors; in fact, I've often heard, "It was hard for me, so why should be easier for the next generation?" These statements are trauma response, simply statements of hurt that have narrowed the windows of resource for some individuals.

I've supported many clients over the years in using a trauma framework to understand the harms committed against entry-level workers, and believe it is my generation's duty to name the doors we hold the keys to—and to support opening these doors with guidance. We may understand that hurt people can hurt others, and so we can understand that healing people heal others. As Latinx social workers, we carry generations of healing in our bodies, we carry wisdom of survival under white supremacy, and lineages of strength and creativity.

Our people are a people of survival in the collective. Social work in the United States has professionalized many of the skills that our families and cultures of origin know are effective in strengthening capacity for survival under the harsh conditions of racial capitalism. As a social worker, whether in training or in the field, I encourage you to examine the skills, capacities, and knowledge that have been passed through you to inform your practice.

ECOLOGIES OF CARE

Ten years after graduating from my MSW program, I recognized that I was curious about clinical practice. In graduate school, I had followed my passion for organizing people as a means of building power at the base for change and had spent a decade working in direct community practice with LGBQ identified youth and trans and gender non-conforming BIPOC young adults aging out of foster care. This work was incredible, joyful, heartbreaking, and deeply embedded in the belief that we need each other to survive at the margins.

I worked at the frontlines of many systems, including psychiatric, carceral, housing, and public assistance. The precarity created by all of these violent systems was incredibly difficult to witness. Increasingly, I questioned the care clients were getting when they returned from therapy, and stated that their therapists didn't acknowledge the pain of systemic violence, didn't have language for naming racism, or had minimized the harm endured during an inpatient psychiatric stay.

I became interested in transitioning from larger agency work to clinical practice and realized I had no idea where to begin. I began asking people I knew who were licensed for advice, I found a clinic in my neighborhood, and slowly made a transition to seeing clients individually after months of guidance from the clinic director, a queer Latino.

It took me six months to make the transition, as I determined how I would pay for my own health insurance and lined up multiple part-time jobs to support myself while working to accumulate my licensing hours. I worked three jobs while accumulating my hours, frequently defaulting on my health insurance payments and maintaining an incredibly high level of stress. I was driven to get my license and to one day offer anti-oppressive, queer-centered psychotherapeutic services—and the cost of this was to my body and my own mental health.

My story is NOT unique. The licensing process is one developed from the core values of capitalism and predicated on scarcity, individualism, and irrational conditions for work and healing. While my work with clients became stronger, my own access to wellness was strained and often out of reach.

I am struck by how many clinicians share this story with me, and these are disproportionally clinicians of color. Because of collective crowd sourcing, I was able to co-sign a small office lease to begin seeing clients. Through collective fundraising and the mentorship of one Latina therapist (Leslie Garcia, I am forever grateful!), I was able to imagine and also support a vision of opening Amanecer, Feminist Psychotherapy.

The last four years have shown me just how difficult the path toward autonomy of practice is for clinicians who are not raised wealthy (classist), who carry student loan debt, and who need consistent access to health insurance (ableist). I offer to anyone who asks, detailed support, instruction, and transparency regarding opening a therapy practice and sustaining the self. What is mine, is ours—and there is no winning in gatekeeping.

As a person deeply connected to nature, I understand the density of an ecology that creates abundance and plenty. Robin Wall Kimmerer writes about the principle of "the honorable harvest," the idea that we should not take more than what we need. What if we applied this principle to the structures that surround mental health care provision? How might we create what I am calling new "fee ecologies," financial structures that support BIPOC clinicians in training (and beyond) through directly addressing historical disproportionality, creative use of those with wealth to share/redistribute, and complex pay structures that ask the most of those who have it, and the least of those who do not?

As social workers we have a duty to continue to imagine and to break through old structures to determine what may meet the needs of communities in more contemporary ways. I believe our work as social workers is to challenge status quo, and to find each other in collective power.

We are a huge profession; we work in all sectors, public and private, and carry great power in the numbers and knowledge we bring to institutions. My hope is that as we watch the veil lift more publicly regarding health care, racial disparities, and structural white supremacy, that we answer a call toward abolition of the police state- and include radically re-examining our roles in "care" as an additional means to un-doing the damages we have contributed to for so long.

Since the very beginning of my path toward this profession, I have held the belief that we must change what is no longer working. My vision is a vision that includes everyone—that we all get to have what we need without the belief that we must take it from each other.

REFLECTION

We are living through a global pandemic and watching the growing impact of the harms of capitalism. There is simply just too much evidence that our systems aren't working for the majority of people. Social workers are on the frontlines of the collapses of these systems, and we too are impacted.

I strongly encourage each of us to find our people, to find those that we can build with. Maybe it is building a new program, a new group, new strategy for care, a new policy to protect workers, or a new union. We the workers must build it.

I am excited to contribute to this book, in hopes that this chapter reaches you at the right moment, when you've had a spark within you that is looking to light up another.   T h e pandemic has taught us all intense lessons for survival and the creative potential for new ways of engaging with each other. We need each other. Go find your people in this work. We have always been and always will be a people of great movement and vision. *Pa'lante, mi gente.*

ABOUT THE AUTHOR

Amelia Ortega, LCSW, currently works as a somatic psychotherapist, organizational change consultant, and professor of Social Work practice. As a social worker, Amelia has worked for the last fourteen years dedicated to supporting queer and trans young adults and families. Amelia currently works in their NYC-based practice, Amanecer Feminist Psychotherapy, and is an instructor at the Columbia University School of Social Work, where they have taught for nine years. Amelia specializes in trauma focused therapies and trauma informed classroom pedagogies. Amelia's clinical and teaching practice engages healing through use of somatic experiencing, EMDR, and their training in the Trauma Conscious Yoga Method. In 2019, Amelia was named by Negocios Now as one of "NYC's 40 Latinos under 40" for their trauma therapy work with LGBTQ Latinx community.

Amelia received their MSW from the Columbia University School of Social Work in 2007, and is beginning work on their doctorate of social welfare at SUNY Buffalo in Fall 2021.

Amelia is a deep listener of all life, and when they aren't working, is often found out in nature with birds and wildlife. They are a photographer, writer, visual creator, and naturalist.

Amelia Ortega, LCSW
Amanecer Feminist Psychotherapy
amanecercounselingervices@gmail.com
IG: @feminist_psychotherapy
LinkedIn: amelia-ortega-lcsw

IT WAS ALL A DREAM!

ANDRES GOMEZ, MSW

I wanted to share my story of a Latino male in the field of social work, with the hope that my words can inspire future Latinos to want to follow their heart and make a difference. I have learned a lot in my life, and typically had the wise words of a Latina to help me learn. These words are in honor of my wife, grandma, mother, and my daughter Julia; three powerful Latinas and a powerful Latina in training!

My road to social work began at a very young age. I was raised by a single mother, who taught her two boys that education is a foundation that cannot be broken. My mother was born in Colombia and immigrated to the United States when she was just a child. My mother put herself through college and earned her master's degree in social work at Fordham University before I was born. She worked for the Board of Education in New York for over thirty years, retiring in 2017.

Watching my own real-life superhero was why I chose the field of social work—or some may say the field chose me. I have always liked working with young people. Growing up, I found roles as a coach, camp counselor in after schools or church, or in sports. I was not only able to be my authentic self, but I was able to connect and allow those young people to be their authentic selves.

As I continued in my education, I attended college and then went into my master's program at The University of Stony Brook. As I was entering this career, I remember asking, "What is the toughest job a social worker could have?" The answer that was shared was to work at a foster care agency. So, there I was, twenty-two, and my first professional job was as a case manager working with families in some of the toughest neighborhoods in Queens and Brooklyn.

I remember my first case: it was a Spanish-speaking mother who had her teen daughter removed because she was left unsupervised. I was asked to work with this family because they were Spanish-speaking, and the foster mother shared that this mother would put lies into her daughter's head. I sat there during their first visit in over a couple of months. I remember the birth mother sharing to her daughter that she was working hard to have her come home. I was heartbroken that this family was torn apart. Something about this family triggered me. I saw my relationship with my mother. I struggled with the complex duality of my role; "Go in there and tell us what is happening" vs. "Support the client and advocate." I went home and cried, and would do that for the next six months.

From abuse to neglect, I would hear horrible stories of

families ripped apart or young people's lives changed forever because of an adult. I sat there at times listening to these stories and wanting to fix or help every family, but at times feeling hopeless. I remember the eyes of every young person, and seeing hope and joy disappear. I remember thinking, how can I help bring hope and joy back into their eyes.

"IF THE GAME SHAKES ME OR BREAKS ME, I HOPE IT MAKES ME A BETTER MAN."

As an undergrad, college was not easy. I struggled in school and learned what failure looked like. I had college advisors share that maybe this was too difficult, and would continue to provide bad advice. I was embarrassed to share with my mom that school was not working out, but I did not know what to do next. I did not want to let her down, and used that as motivation to turn things around. I was actually able to graduate on time!

I applied and was accepted to graduate school while working full-time at the foster care agency. I went to school in the evening and was committed to finishing my program in two years. In most of my classes, I represented two minority groups in social work: I was Latino and a man. I would always be asked for my perspective, as if I was speaking for all Latino men. I hoped I'd said the right words and didn't offend anyone. I always felt like I stood out like a sore thumb because I was not like most of my classmates. I sure was tested by them, but what they didn't know was that I had a secret weapon.

They didn't know that I was raised by two powerful

superhumans that were both women. I was blessed to be raised by my mother and grandmother. I learned strength, respect, and the powerful tool of overcoming adversity. So, while I got tested in class, what they didn't know was I had been practicing for most of my life. I was blessed to have my grandmother see me graduate with a master's degree in social work before she passed away. I was thankful for all the lessons and conversations with *mi abuela*. She taught me hard work, resilience, and hope, and I would carry her lessons in conversations in every interaction I would have moving forward.

"YOU KNOW VERY WELL WHO YOU ARE, DON'T LET 'EM HOLD YOU DOWN, REACH FOR THE STARS."

After I earned my degree, I left my job at the foster care agency, wanting to make more of an impact. I applied at a small nonprofit starting out in New York (but originally founded in Boston). This organization's mission was to empower young people to find their true potential by preparing for meaningful careers in business and technology.

I remember visiting the program during my interview phase and was shocked to see so many smiling positive faces. To be honest, coming from working at the foster care system, I wasn't used to that. *This place must be some sort of scam,* I thought. In what world can students from some of the toughest neighborhoods in New York prepare for jobs in corporate America in six months? I guess in this world. I got the job, and began my career as a social worker at a job training program.

As I started to meet with students, I realized they had the same look I saw several years ago in the foster care agency. I knew it would be my job and mission to bring hope and confidence back into those eyes. There are so many oppressions and systematic barriers in our society; the world needs more social workers. The world needs more superheroes.

So, my job was to help remove barriers and connect students to resources so they can start their careers. Easy job, right? Well, what I learned from these young people was how much trauma they have been through in their lives. What I also learned was that these students needed to have a trusting adult that would listen, be consistent, and see them as the high-value talent that they are.

I didn't realize at the time, but I had been preparing for this role. So, I listened, I tried my hardest to be consistent, and I recognized that each amazing individual already had the ability to overcome any future challenges because of the grit they already developed. Student after student, I would use my humor to engage, my empathy to absorb, and my social work skills to problem solve. Students started to open up, and I could see the hope come back to their eyes. It was working!

I have worked thirteen years at this organization, and I can still remember the narrative of almost every young person that has walked through these doors. I am blessed our lives crossed, and if even for a short time, I was able to help these students get hope back into their eyes then I did my job.

MY LEGACY

Growing up in New York, I was used to moving and doing that, I never stopped to think about what I have done or where I have been. This last year has made me think even more not only about how precious life is, but also what I want my legacy to be. My wish is that I inspired someone, put a smile on someone's face, or helped to put hope back in someone's eyes.

Three years ago, I took a new position that led me to leave the New York office that I worked in for over ten years. All I wanted was to spend time with the graduates before I left. My organization hosted an event after work, and student after student showed up. Some graduates had not been back to the office for over ten years. We had a good time that evening, reminiscing about conversations and sharing stories about what they have done since graduating. A couple of alums pulled me aside and said thank you. In the field of social work, there are times when you see the immediate impact, and many more times when you don't always see the impact. Those "thank yous" that evening were the impact. I saw the hope in their eyes, and was blessed that our paths had crossed.

I spent over ten years learning how to be a parent by watching my amazing students navigate full-time school, work, and for many of them, full-time parenting. I held many beautiful babies in my arms, as their parent chose a path to self-sustainability. I learned from my students. Growing up, I never knew what Father's Day was. We never needed to celebrate. As a first-time father myself, I am excited to celebrate Father's

Day with Julia, and share with her all that I have learned from watching my students.

REFLECTION

Social work has been an important part of my professional career, and some may say a part of my identity. I have learned so much during my social work career. I have laughed, cried, and I have been inspired by the incredible young people that I have had the great fortune to serve and support. Being a social worker is hard work. It has been a bunch of long hours, blood, sweat, and tears. We are so focused on others' pain that we at times do not understand our own pain. I have been traumatized, and I am still healing. That said, I would not change my profession for the world. I have learned a lot about myself, and find joy in helping to change others' lives and impacting systematic oppressions in our society.

For those that are interested in entering the field of social work as a career, I leave you with these three tips: #1 Find the hardest role or job you can as a social worker to start. I chose to work at a foster care agency, and those were some of the toughest lessons I learned. #2 Find mentors. I am blessed to have met many amazing people in my career, and three that I call mentors. When facing many personal and professional challenges, I always think about what they would say or do. Thank you Lisette, Gerald, and Jon! #3 Always put the oxygen mask on YOU first. Make it a priority to take care of yourself. It is going to be so important that you develop healthy habits that support your wellbeing.

- Who are the superheroes in your life?
- As a fellow Queens native once said; "With great power comes great responsibilities." What impact do you want to make?
- Find what makes you smile and do it every day!

ABOUT THE AUTHOR

Andres Gomez is the director of enrollment for Year Up Dallas/Fort Worth. He has been with the organization for over thirteen years. In his previous role, he served as the director of student services, overseeing a team of social workers working to navigate student barriers. In his current role, his team is responsible for recruitment of over 250 talented young professionals to enter the corporate workforce each year. Andres does this by working with his team, the community of Dallas, and Dallas College to find talent. His greatest accomplishment was welcoming their largest class in the middle of the pandemic.

Andres received his undergraduate and master's degrees from the University of Stonybrook in Long Island, New York. Growing up in New York City, he recognized that talent is everywhere, but opportunities are not. After working for a foster care agency, he wanted to make more of a lasting impact and joined the Year Up program in the Wall Street area of Manhattan.

Andres moved to the Dallas area in 2018. When he is not helping to close the opportunity divide, Andres enjoys sports, cooking, traveling, and spending time with his wife and newborn daughter Julia.

Andres Gomez
andgomez913@gmail.com
IG: @Workhardhavefun23
718.799.6179

LEARNING IS A LIFELONG JOURNEY

DR. EDITH CHAPARRO, PH.D., LCSW-R

MY INFLUENCERS

As a first-generation American, my legacy is a story of professional growth while sustaining my Latina identity. As early as I am able to remember, I have always felt comfortable helping others, caring for people's feelings, and having empathy. As a result, I've become a strong and loving daughter, wife, sister, mentor, and professional Latina.

My qualities originated from my loving parents, who may not have been perfect, but provided me with the necessary lessons, love, and support to succeed. My journey was not easy. I dealt with the loss of family members throughout my life. My brother died when I was a young teenager, and my father died two years after my wedding. I experienced immense pain and profound sadness from the loss of my brother and father. As a result of my grief, my life became very disrupted and I couldn't even think straight. Many times I felt as though I was not making proper personal or educational decisions—and this was frustrating, emotionally debilitating, and slowed my progress. However, I found the strength to continue—and my journey is certainly not over.

My parents immigrated from Paraguay, South America, in the 1960s, and I was born in the Bronx, New York, in the 70s. As a first-generation American, I greatly value the sacrifice my parents endured in order to provide me with a better life and opportunities that would not be possible if they had remained in their country. After my parents immigrated from Paraguay, their family members did not follow them. Therefore, I was raised without relatives in the United States, leaving me with no choice other than annual trips to connect with them.

Since childhood, I have been curious about Paraguayan culture and would travel to Paraguay to visit my grandmother during summer break from school. I learned to speak Spanish and attempted to learn the Paraguayan native language, Guarani. I enjoyed meeting relatives, developing friendships, and I especially was intrigued by the fascinating culture and belief system. My most wonderful memories were established in Paraguay and I greatly miss my cousins with whom I have a close relationship.

The neighborhood where I was raised lacked diversity and was predominantly White. While attending grammar school and high school, I often felt displaced. Although I established long-standing and solid friendships that were not Latinx, I always remained curious about having Latinx friendships. It was not until I entered college that I encountered Latinx and ethnically diverse classmates. I connected with different Latinx and ethnically diverse classmates in order to sustain my Latina identity.

My college campus did not offer Latinas a sense of unity; therefore in 1997, I united with three like-minded Latina students and we established the first Latina Greek organization on campus, which still thrives today. Being able to identify with Latinas who followed a similar belief system provided me with a sense of alliance and comfort; something I did not experience while growing up.

During my early adulthood, while attending undergraduate school, I voluntarily entered psychotherapy treatment. I had a mission to work towards self-growth before entering a career, serious relationship, or future decision-making. Throughout my therapeutic experience, I noticed many positive changes; such as focusing on my school work, my grades improved, I began establishing meaningful friendships, and I also realized that I wanted to help my community.

In addition to attending therapy, I volunteered as a surgical liaison at a nearby hospital. As months went by, I noticed that the patients wanted more than just concrete services; they needed emotional support. I was able to provide support and assist the patients; this was immensely valuable and gave me a sense of self-fulfillment.

The experience gained from attending therapy and

volunteering provided the foundation for becoming a social worker. While volunteering, I discovered that I was applying several social work core values such as integrity, service, and the importance of human relationships. I applied the ability to empower clients; I demonstrated my commitment while being honest and fair with clients, and I enhanced the well-being of clients.

While volunteering and therapy provided a solid social work basis, my parents greatly influenced the reason I chose a career path in social work. My late father was a physician and owned a private clinic in a predominantly Latinx community for over forty years. I always admired him and dreamed of the ability to serve the Latinx community. I enthusiastically observed his interactions with patients and community members; he taught me strong values such as being responsible, tough, and humble. I cherish the close relationship we had and I wish I could share my current achievements with him.

In addition to my father's influence, I see so much of my mother in me. My mother is very kind, soft-spoken, and has been an outstanding role model. She has always taught me to be kind to others and to help others that are in need. I recall that for her birthday, she would ask her friends to bring cookies and gifts for children instead of for her; she would donate the cookies and gifts to underprivileged children. Her frequent acts of kindness have shown me how to be a better person. My parents' brilliant qualities have contributed to my character both personally and professionally. My mother taught me to be grateful for all that I have, be frugal, and zealously pursue my life goals and education.

Upon graduating with my master's degree in social work, I began to work at my father's clinic, counseling patients. Working at his clinic provided me with the ability to connect with patients, specifically Latinas. Helping patients to identify and address their emotional issues along with empowering them was truly rewarding. In addition to helping patients, my first work experience taught me the importance of cultural awareness and competence. My cultural background and experiences have reinforced my aspiration to serve the Latinx community.

PATHWAY TO SOCIAL WORK

When it was time to select a career path, my goal was to choose a career that would enable me to help others, particularly within the mental health field. My neighbor, a very wise, supportive, and kind woman, provided me with a booklet covering different graduate school programs. As I reviewed the various programs related to mental health services, I reviewed the master's in social work program description, and I instantly felt a connection. The description of the social work program matched precisely with my career aspirations, and at that moment, I felt extremely confident with my choice. I applied to various programs and chose to enroll in New York University's social work master's degree program.

Upon graduating, in May 2003, I was employed at an outpatient mental health center, along with working by my father's side, and simultaneously I began to study for my social work license exam. I knew that without a social work license, I would not be able to secure employment or work independently in private practice. I gathered several textbooks and resources and began to diligently study for my exam. While completing practice exams, I noticed that I was consistently attaining the same score that was not sufficient to pass the exam. I began to develop test-taking strategies and, within a week, my score on practice tests increased a great deal. I was relieved that after several months of intense studying, I finally noticed an improvement. I scheduled my exam, applied the exam strategies and knowledge that I had acquired, and passed my exam with flying colors.

Soon after, I was offered a clinical position at a state hospital and also was able to operate a part-time private practice while under clinical supervision. These opportunities made me realize the importance of licensure.

After sharing my exam preparation experience with colleagues, they informed me of the struggles they were encountering regarding passing their exams. In fact, one colleague was unsuccessful after multiple attempts and had become disillusioned, ready to give up and change careers. I offered to tutor her using the strategies that I had developed. My purpose and intention was to help my colleagues to pass their exams. After all, I knew how much passing the licensure exam meant and how much it changed my professional life.

With my assistance, my colleagues obtained licensure. They were extremely grateful and expressed that without my help, they would not be able to pass the exam. Once they attained their license, they were able to advance in their career, apply for greater employment opportunities, and improve their financial situations.

Around this time, a dear friend and mentor helped me secure an undergraduate teaching position. At first, I was tense and lacked confidence; however, I persevered and succeeded as an adjunct professor. I felt comfortable and it was rewarding lecturing my students. In some ways, teaching and providing psychotherapy is similar. They both have comparable skill sets such as: educating clients, listening to their needs, providing feedback, and empowering them to reach their goals. As a result, my clinical training allowed me to become an effective educator.

WHERE I PRESENTLY STAND

I am very grateful for the tremendous support I continuously receive from my family and husband which have allowed me to reach my professional aspirations. Also, a combination of skills, experience, perseverance, integrity, and bravery led me to where I am today professionally. Because of my team and professional experiences, I developed an educational program to assist social workers to pass their license exams, and I've dedicated myself to this mission for the past fifteen years.

Teaching social workers to pass the exam is only half the work; I dedicate time to listen to their trials and tribulations related to passing their exam. I have observed and extensively researched different factors that may be impacting their ability to pass the social work license exam. I continue to constantly learn from the multitude of social workers that I come across. In addition, I am keenly aware of the diverse population of social workers I am working with and how important they are to the social work field.

As a Latina social worker, I consider myself an educator, mentor, and liaison. My professional community consists of mental health clinicians, specifically a diverse population of social workers, Latinx professionals, and graduate students. Building a solid community of like-minded Latinas creates a ripple effect that positively affects those who need us most—our clients and the communities we serve.

My vision and focus is to leave a lasting impact by empowering social workers and other professionals to reach their full potential. By sharing my knowledge and experience with Latinas, my goal is to mold them into competent, brave, fierce, and successful mental health professionals. I wish to leave a legacy of creating success, opportunities and being an integral part of shaping the next generation of powerful professional women.

REFLECTION

When I first began my career, the social work field was not very well established in terms of licensure. Fortunately, over time the social work field has gained a tremendous amount of recognition and respect. With ever-increasing diversity, the social work profession has become critical in meeting the needs of a wide range of patient populations. Presently, the social work field consists of assisting individuals and families on a micro-level and a macro-level, by identifying injustices and working towards positive social change. Furthermore, mental health is highly recognized and has become accepted as an important and much-needed part of daily life. The rise of the social work field will continue, and I am thankful to witness these positive changes and to have the ability to participate in the evolution of the profession.

- What steps can you take to form an alliance with like-minded Latinas?
- What are your fears, and how can you challenge yourself to overcome these fears?
- What choices are you making now that could positively impact your future?

ABOUT THE AUTHOR

Dr. Edith Chaparro is a licensed clinical social worker and a practicing psychologist dedicated to delivering the highest quality client services for the past twenty years. In addition, she is the owner and creator of the influential Social Work Exam Prep Bootcamp, which has been assisting social workers nationally to obtain their professional licenses for the past fifteen years. Dr. Chaparro's work has been dedicated to advocating and helping culturally diverse communities at both the clinical treatment level and the academic level.

Dr. Chaparro holds a doctorate degree in counseling psychology from Walden University, where she dedicated years towards research related to factors that impact license exam performance. In addition, she holds a master's in clinical social work from New York University. During her career, she has been a private practitioner, clinical supervisor, adjunct professor, business owner, and mentor. She currently serves as an executive committee member and member at large for the National Association of Social Workers (NASW)-NYC chapter and has served as the chairperson of the NASW-NYC Nominations Committee. Dr. Chaparro has earned numerous awards throughout her career and is regularly invited to be a guest lecturer at various universities and well-known organizations.

Dr. Edith Chaparro, Ph.D., LCSW-R
socialworkbootcamp@gmail.com
IG: @socialworkexambootcamp
917-683-8601

LOST IN TRANSITION

LUISA LOPEZ, MSW

TRANSITIONS

One of my favorite ways to think about the profession of social work is that we are in the business of "transition." Change is hard; behavioral change, social change, institutional or structural change—Social workers serve as the transitional brokers for individuals, organizations, and governments, as a sort of lubricant that keeps the gears of the social compact well oiled and running. Managing the **chaos** of transitions from young to old, from simple tolerance to welcoming acceptance, and from nebulous ideas of diversity and inclusion to creating spaces that value, encourage, and promote equity is an act that requires moral and mental clarity from those of us charged with finding solutions to the world's most pressing issues.

The ability to find comprehensive, societal solutions, to adapt, and to help individuals and groups along in their own transitions *within* these systems—*that* is a social worker's **superpower**. We are duty bound to empower individuals, organizations, and entire communities, and to help them thrive within the inhospitable spaces fostered by these systems of oppression.

Deriving order and finding harmony beyond the chaos that systemic forces wreak on an individual, a family, an organization, or a community, and finding profound meaning in that challenging (and often times invisible) work, has been a driving force for me as I've navigated my career and my life as a social worker. Life can be challenging for all of us; I have found that unleashing the power of transition within myself is the key to making a real difference in other's lives, as well. My life so far has been a master class on the art of transitions, finding order (and my way) among the chaos and obstacles designed to test my resolve and my commitment to finding out what kind of force I want to be in this world.

CHAOS

During my early days as a social worker, I came across a wide spectrum of people that had seemingly been pulled out of my own history growing up in Washington Heights: single moms, hovering below the poverty line; young men battling substance use disorder; new immigrant families facing the challenges of raising teenagers in wildly different circumstances than in their home countries. In all of those spaces, I was acutely aware of how my clients were counting on me to help them through these transitions and challenges, and to somehow alleviate the stress in a way that made sense for them.

Nothing in my social work education could have

prepared me for the overwhelming sense of duality that came to characterize my experiences when I returned to my old neighborhood to serve my community. Wrapped up in the joy and pride I felt at providing culturally respectful, family-centered services, there was also a constant battle to accept that this *essential* work was HARD.

For someone who values excellence and careful attention to detail, maintaining a work standard that reflected these values was paramount. However, it proved nearly impossible to do when faced with measuring outcomes and goals, assessment deadlines, and grueling home visit schedules. In a community where a vast majority of residents were constantly experiencing one crisis situation after another, managing performance targets was an unrealistic objective, and led to increased pressure. The chaos cultivated by weak support systems that left an entire community with diminished access to resources, jobs, education, and opportunities had created an unsustainable environment which produced anxiety and left me questioning my ability to serve my community competently. Was I resilient enough? Was I strong enough to shoulder these burdens, both for myself and for my clients?

Around the same time, the chaos of my work would find a way to follow me home—my husband and I were diagnosed with unexplained infertility. I didn't know then how learning that I may never have children would impact my social work practice and my life. To be a Latina in this world is to carry with you the innumerable expectations that come with that, and no expectation looms larger or heavier than that of motherhood. What did this turn of events mean for me, for my family, and for my future? Where do I fit into to the landscape of my life if I can't even do the most basic thing a person should be able to do? And the cruelest question of all: what kind of sad twist of fate is it to be charged with the care and support of your community, but be unable to create a family to care for and support? Navigating these questions during that particular time is one of the hardest and most challenging things I've ever had to do, all the while holding space for clients and supporting them through their own challenges.

ORDER

During this time, I decided to view my work as a social worker as a lifeline, and as a balm for my troubled soul. There was a distinct pleasure in reaching termination with a client, after successfully helping them access the support they needed; I felt a beaming rush of pride when my clients attained their GED, or successfully applied for permanent work. The "work" became a critical space, where helping people through the transitions in their lives allowed me to transition and adapt into the reality of living life with the major disruption that is infertility. So much of struggling with infertility comes with a sense that life is "on hold"—the universe keeps moving the line until the next injection, the next appointment, the next sonogram, or the next cycle. My work was the one place where everything kept moving, wheels kept spinning, and I could have a tangible, positive effect on those around me.

During this time, I also began my work with the Latino Social Work Coalition and Scholarship Fund (the very same organization I now lead), which is dedicated to increasing the number of culturally and linguistically competent social workers, and providing financial support for Latinx social work students. The Latino Social Work Coalition provided me the opportunity to get my first taste of nonprofit leadership and legislative advocacy, giving me the opportunity to speak about the importance of our mission and to advocate on behalf of our scholarship program. Creating and fostering a pipeline for culturally humble social workers to lead the charge in providing healing-centered and trauma-focused services to address systemic inequalities is the cornerstone of our mission and our work.

This was a natural extension of my work with families, and where I got to experience the value of powerful advocacy, and how it translates into tangible support for those that need it the most. Once again, the universe had placed me in a space where I could smooth the life transitions of countless people (in this case, social work students), by helping them get much needed financial support and assistance. It was powerful work that would lay the groundwork for my future—and that of the organization itself.

HARMONY

I believe that finding peace within the chaos of life is a gift, and that no struggle comes into one's life without there being a higher purpose learning behind it. Throughout my personal and professional trajectory, I have found my higher purpose, which is to advocate and make space for people like me, Latinas like me, infertility warriors like me, social workers like me.

My time providing clinical services to my community set the ground work for my decision to delve deeper into the waters of legislative advocacy, which is the work that would deeply impact my life and the trajectory of my career. While working as a policy fellow in Congress in Washington, D.C. I learned to recognize the vital importance of policy development and implementation in creating and supporting the structural change that is so needed in marginalized communities like my own, and how the decisions made at the federal level have a deep impact on how issues that plague our most vulnerable communities, such as homelessness, poverty, the opioid crisis, and education equity and access, are handled at the local level.

At that same time, I began taking baby steps (pun intended) toward what would become a driving force in all that I do: advocating on behalf of those impacted by infertility, especially for equal access to family-building resources and support for women of color. Systemic inequality found a way to impact even my desire to expand my family, with low-income and less-educated people having less access to the resources necessary to consider artificial reproductive technology as an option.

I began my advocacy to ensure equal access to all family building options for people experiencing infertility or other reproductive disorders. Infertility is an expensive drain on your resources, on your mental health, on your body, and on your relationships. There are but a few spaces to openly to discuss these things, and for the most part they are not open, accessible, or welcoming to Black and women of color. For so long, I had dedicated myself to advocating for others, and elevating spaces that allowed people to lift up their voices to empower themselves and their communities. Now here was the chance to advocate for myself and my own struggles, to address the fears and deep sense of disappointment with my fertility journey, and to once again create a space where other women of color similar to me could speak openly about this profoundly personal issue. I didn't have all the answers (social workers never do), but here was a chance to use my own experience to let others know that they were not alone. My professional life and my personal life had now come full circle, and I was adapting the skills I had long used to help others, now to also jumpstart my own leadership journey as an advocate to promote social change around issues that I deeply care about.

Finding the commonalities between my advocacy on behalf of those experiencing infertility and on behalf of social workers has been one of the great gifts of my journey. Now more than ever, the advocacy of the Latino Social Work Coalition is paramount to address the imminent shortage of social workers to meet the demand for our services. Often, I am the only social worker in the room, and I consider it my duty to consider the perspectives of those most directly impacted when addressing the pressing issues of the day. It is said that, "those closest to the problem are closest to the solution"; as such, I believe it is the duty of those in the social work profession to elevate and make space for the very people we are here to support. The same way I continue to show up, and speak up for the experiences of those experiencing infertility, I bring that same passion, stamina, resilience, and confidence to my work advocating for students, and (naturally) to ease the *transition* of this mighty organization into the future.

My social work journey has been an incredibly fulfilling one, and has served as a roadmap with which to navigate all the cornerstones of my personal and professional life—through my work supporting my clients in marginalized communities; by creating a space for Latinx people experiencing the pain of infertility; to now advocating on behalf of Latinx social workers everywhere, I have managed what years ago seemed impossible: find my way through the chaos of life and into harmony that only peace can bring.

REFLECTION

The lives of social work professionals can often be engulfed by the challenges our clients and communities are navigating. Learning about and finding space to explore our own areas of advocacy, and deciding which issues are of paramount importance to us can often be a challenge. I encourage you to decide what is important to you, and which injustices you can alleviate by lending your voice.

- As you look around, which issues are you drawn to and feel you can contribute to?

- When you take inventory of your life, what are the times that you felt most powerful and were able to speak up? Why?

- Where is your community of likeminded peers that can help you navigate issues you feel passionately about? Find them!

- What skills do you have (or can you work on) to better assist you in your advocacy?

ABOUT THE AUTHOR

Luisa Lopez, MSW is a native of New York City and currently serves as President of the Latino Social Work Coalition and Scholarship Fund, and Director of Digital Media at the Office of the Manhattan Borough President. She has previously served as chief of staff at the NYC Council, and served in the Washington, DC office of former Congressman José E. Serrano as a policy fellow with a focus on addressing community issues in the South Bronx.

In her career, she has concentrated on addressing structural challenges by developing and implementing social interventions aimed at effecting positive change at all levels of government. Additionally, Luisa has become an advocate for the increased accessibility and availability of assisted reproductive technology, as well as destigmatizing infertility in communities of color.

As president of the Latino Social Work Coalition she is a fierce advocate for increasing the number of culturally and linguistically competent social workers serving in New York City's most vulnerable communities, as well as for the importance and value that social workers bring to all areas of public life and civic engagement.

Luisa holds B.A. in political science from the College of the Holy Cross. A social worker by training, Luisa earned her Masters of Social Work from the New York University Silver School of Social Work.

Luisa Lopez

luisa@lopeznyc.com

IG: @Lopez.CoMedia, @LuisaLopezNYC

929-352-1094

WHEN OIL DOWN MET SANCOCHO

PAULA MCMILLAN-PEREZ, LCSW

WHY DOES THE TURTLE RETREAT INTO ITS SHELL?

When I think of the word identity, one of the first thoughts that comes to me is how many meanings it has carried for me from childhood until the present day. As a child, I learned the definition because it was a vocabulary word in school and it was on a spelling test—and I did very well on spelling tests. This was something that I was proud of, because doing well in school was as much the expectation as it was the reality of being the child of a Caribbean parent.

My mother, who immigrated to this country from the island of Grenada in 1967, knew that a good education opens doors. It was rooted in my identity for as long as I could remember. This was something that I openly accepted. But what I would learn is that acceptance in other areas would not come easy.

In elementary school, I found it challenging to connect with the people who looked like me. If I am honest, I didn't really realize the "why" until high school. I realized that I was viewed as different because I looked different, I spoke differently, I dressed differently, I was smart, and had perfect attendance. That was embarrassing.

A public elementary school in the North Bronx can feel like a jungle; a jungle with asphalt to play on during recess, with a daily battle for the last chocolate milk, and one that is hard to navigate with a single immigrant parent working hard to make ends meet. Not having the same access as your peers to the latest sneakers, video game consoles, or clothing that some of the other kids had felt hard on top of the cultural piece when you have a parent that grew up with less and found ways to be creative.

I was marginalized for being smart and speaking eloquently because the thought was only white people are smart. I was called Oreo. I felt lonely and the jokes were painful. They were always the same. "You sound like a white girl," "Stop talking like a white girl," or "You think you are better than us when you talk like you're white."

Unfortunately, during this time, public schools in The Bronx had a lack of resources in the way of updated textbooks, counselors, affordable enrichment, and afterschool programs, which allow children to succeed at higher levels. I internalized this experience because I felt shame and confusion about why this seemed to be only happening to me. I felt as though I was less than because of the treatment I received from kids. When

I shared how I was feeling with my mother, like many mothers she told me it would pass. The feelings didn't pass, so all I was left with was hurt.

Thinking back, what hurt the most was other Black girls who made fun of my natural hair, which was braided by my mother or sister. Now let me be clear: these were not the "cool braids with the beads and bubbles" that some of you may remember from the early nineties (if you weren't alive yet, feel free to Google it); these were the random "this hair needs to last the week" braids or "three quick braids" because we have to run out the door to make it on time to school.

Having chemically relaxed hair gave you (at least what I thought in my mind as an elementary school kid) access to an elite club of Black girls that I desperately wanted access to, but between my natural hair and non-name-brand wardrobe, I didn't make it. Being told over numerous years that the only reason I earned good grades is that "I wanted to be white, that's why I talked like them" or being called "Math book" because the company who made the math textbooks at that time were MacMillan Learning, which only had one letter different than my last name. Don't even get me started on having the last name McMillan; it was a source of joy for my peers to tease me over.

WHAT BOX DO I CHECK OFF?

I had about two close friends and a handful of others who were more like acquaintances, but as human development went, I desired that level of acceptance in my elementary school brain.

I also desired to not feel condemned because I spoke how I was taught at home, or because I was well-read and often looked up words I didn't understand.

The most hurtful part for me was was when I helped others who were struggling, but when these same peers were around others, they would act as if I did not exist. Some of us do not have the language to communicate these feelings that come up in our bodies or a support system to help us navigate these social constructs that exist.

What was interesting about this (as I began reflecting on these experiences as I aged) was that as a kid I didn't realize it, but what I would figure out later is that I always felt comfortable with Latinx students. My elementary school mind recognized that I felt like I could be myself, I wasn't teased about my hair but rather I could talk about it.

The first time I learned about the beauty supply store and products for textured hair was from girls at the lunch table who identified as Dominican and Puerto Rican. I wasn't teased or taunted about the way I spoke, but rather asked what certain words meant or asked if something was being pronounced or spelled correctly as some were English Language Learners and did not always feel comfortable asking others. It was as if a door that I never knew existed opened for me because I felt as though I finally found my people.

As the years progressed in middle school and then high school, I realized that there were so many similarities between the Grenadian culture I was raised in and the cultures of friends from Puerto Rico and The Dominican Republic. Having an "old school" Mom, I was not able to go to other people's homes for visits or have sleepovers. She used to say, "You have your own home and your own bed to sleep in." As frustrated as I was with those types of responses, I wasn't in a developmental place to understand the cultural implications of why this wasn't as common as it was for my more American peers. Can you imagine the trouble I got into for sucking my teeth and rolling my eyes when she said those things?

Many of my Latinx friends understood and were able to commiserate with me. This helped with the feelings of social isolation that happen as a young adult beginning to figure out individuality. Growing into your identity can feel like a strange thing. To be the first generation born in the U.S. comes with its own set of nuances that have no handbook. Even if there was a handbook, we know that there is no one size fits all, but it was my goal to find things that could be common, which led me to one of my favorite things: food!

RACE VS. IDENTITY OR IDENTIFICATION?

No matter the country, language, or culture, all people get together and share stories, company, laughter, joy, and sorrow with food. In Grenada, there is a dish (actually it is the national dish) called Oil Down that is a delicious mix of many things that include breadfruit, salted meat, chicken, dumplings, callaloo, and other vegetables, all stewed in coconut milk, herbs, and spices to make a hearty and flavorful one-pot meal. It is called oil down because the coconut milk simmers down and releases its rich flavored oil into the pot. Sometimes the process of making it takes many hands doing their part to get all the ingredients together, so it is also an event. This reminded me so much of the time that I was taught how to make Dominican Sancocho, which is also considered to be a national dish, but admittedly there are many members of the Latinx community who have a history with it. But I was taught that is a stew with seven different types of meat cooked together with root vegetables and served over white rice with avocado.

Oil Down meets Sancocho is the way I describe my merging identities based on these experiences, because these two dishes are literal and figurative representations of the mixing and melting pot that we live in and are navigating through to find our people, our pieces of meat and vegetables. Those pieces make up a savory, satisfying, and fulfilling meal. A meal that you look forward to on special occasions with special people, as you share your stories and experiences all while reliving those close to you from the times in the past.

Our identities, just like chefs in the kitchen, create different flavors of stew. The one thing that is the same is the merging of our identities; it makes for a delicious melting pot with many things to offer. As an Afro-Caribbean who also identifies as Latinx based on friends who became family, marrying a Latinx man, and hopefully God willing one day being a mother to a Latinx child, it was especially important to me to be able to identify that our identity is not just one neat thing that fits easily into a box. I do not fit into a box, nor do my identity or my values. Identity is many things; it is messy, it is confusing, it can make you feel just as much rejection as much as it can make you feel acceptance. It is what and who you identify as and with. Only you can make that decision and distinction.

As we age, (especially women of color in my experience) it is not the easiest thing to reach out and ask for help or admit that we cannot do something. I admit that I struggled with this, and at times continue to, but one of the few things that I am certain of in this life is that it becomes so much richer and so much more meaningful when you have the support of those around you, not just to share it with, but to lean on or catch you when you fall, to lend a helping hand, to cheer for your accomplishments, wipe away your tears, or just sit with you in silence to know that you are not alone.

I admit that there are some who have a whole network of friends and family that fit this mold, some have a person and some do not identify as having anyone for various reasons. This is just one of the many things that led me to fall in love with the social work profession. It reminds me of my beloved Oil Down and Sancocho with the mixing of different ingredients that create a rich flavorful mixture that brings so many together. It allows for memory creation over these savory meals, sharing stories, laughter, teaching younger generations how to create these dishes, and watching over time how they are able to craft it into their own while maintaining the integrity of the initial dish.

Yes, I have had oil down that was too dry and sancocho that

was too salty, but it never stopped me from going back and trying again with food that touches my soul, the same way that I cannot imagine what my life would be at this moment had I engaged in other work. Little elementary school me wouldn't have believed it because the first counselors and social workers she met were White. Middle school me and high school me weren't much different. But I would end up becoming the difference I needed to see in my community, and be the person for those who had questions that they didn't know who to go to for answers. Be what it is you want to see.

REFLECTION

Anyone who doesn't have a clear understanding of the scope of what a social worker does and why we have such a great and growing need for this profession, I encourage you to come speak with us. Ask us questions, allow us to partner with you. Look at the ways that the COVID-19 pandemic has shed greater light on what is happening in our nation with respect to racial themes and marginalized communities in ways that have carved a path for people in ways they had not before.

We NEED Black Indigenous People of Color, young people, artists, activists, educators, attorneys, and community members that are invested. We NEED career changers. We need people who look and sound like us doing this work, empowering others, uplifting communities, infusing cultural competence, equity, and social justice into practice—and into our reality. As you read the many stories in this book and get to know snippets of the authors' lives and careers, please explore which resonate with you and why. Explore what themes resonate with you in relation to those experiences and reflect on why they matter. Reflect on all of the wonderful reasons why you matter.

- Describe what words of encouragement you might tell your younger self to support them through their process of identity exploration.
- What is a physical representation of your own identity that you believe is important to pass down to future generations?

ABOUT THE AUTHOR

Paula McMillan-Perez is an Afro-Caribbean licensed social worker, coach, and framework mentor who was raised and resides in the Bronx, NY. A graduate of Mt. Saint Mary College majoring in psychology and human service, she earned a Bachelor of Art as well as is a graduate of Adelphi University earning a Master of Social Work degree, she also obtained a certification as a professional coach from the Life Coach Institute. She has over a decade of experience serving all age groups surrounding child welfare, forensic social work, substance abuse, and trauma.

Through her work in New York City communities, she saw a need to create more accessible services for people of color, women, and children, which is how Personalize Your Coaching, LLC was born! Partnering with educators, individuals, and organizations to enhance confidence, communication, and build better relationships to move from surviving to thriving is what this work is all about. Through individual coaching, courses, group coaching, and workshop facilitation, she supports clients' holistic growth through a mental wellness lens ensuring the capability to reach their goals.

Paula enjoys spending time with her husband JR, exploring and eating all over NYC, traveling, practicing self-care, playing video games, and reading comic books.

Paula McMillan-Perez

paula@personalizeyourcoaching.life

IG: personalizeyourcoaching

FB: personalizeyourcoachingllc

347.601.4670

Madrina

CONTRA VIENTO Y MAREA

DR. ROSA M. GIL, DSW

"As a social worker we need to integrate the cultural competency into whatever domain of social work."

When thinking back over my years in the field of social work, I must acknowledge the influence of Paolo Freire, a Brazilian educator who was a brilliant thinker. Through his book, *Pedagogy of the Oppressed,* which I have read many times, he helped me to look closely at what seems to be the reality, but is not.

He focused on the illiterate, the powerless people, to understand how we could make a difference. His whole theoretical structure is based on peeling the layers back, empowering the individual to find out who she/he is, and what the circumstances are that are impacting his or her life. It also means looking at what their rights are and being comfortable, demanding that they be acknowledged and respected.

Freire is very clear about the issue of the power position and the down position, and understanding each position in the relationship. Who is holding the power—the therapist, the social worker, or the individual—and when will the individual be given the opportunity to have power when they are in the down position?

For me, during my training as a social worker, when I finished my master's degree, when I did post-graduate training in psychotherapy, during my years in private practice and over fifty years in policy and executive management positions in social welfare, health delivery system, academia and economic development, Freire has been there in the daily work, helping me to look at what is beyond reality.

GROWING UP IN CUBA

I grew up in Santiago, Cuba, a small island off the coast of Florida that has been a thorn in the side of the U.S. for the last sixty-five years. The city is on the southern coast, near Guantanamo Bay, and has a population of 500,000. It has a small community feeling, and is surrounded by mountains.

I grew up loving to play outside, and went to Catholic schools taught by French nuns. I was young when I was first exposed to French, and began learning both English and French.

Our society was one where family communication was important, and we were very much interconnected with friends and family. *"Familismo"* was more important than individualism, and I was very lucky to grow up in the same household with my grandmother.

My family was middle class. My father was born in Spain and came to work in Cuba with his brothers when he was twelve years old. He lost his father before he was born and his mother at birth. He had no formal education whatsoever. My mother was also born in Spain, and her family were immigrants who had a lot of struggles.

FROM PHYSICIAN TO SOCIOLOGY

I had the benefit of three generations living in our home, and I remember talking to my family at dinner about wanting to choose science as the area of concentration for my high school studies. I wanted to choose science because I was interested in being a physician. My father said, "Women are not doctors. Do you know any doctor who is a woman?" I stuck with my choice, and eventually, he asked a doctor friend of his to take me into an operating room. It only lasted five minutes, because when I saw all the blood, I fainted.

As it turned out, I went into science, but with the idea that I would attend Villanueva University in Havana to be a psychologist. As I reflected later, these experiences gave me a coping mechanism where, if you have a goal and there are barriers in your way, you should not give it up.

GROWING UP DURING A REVOLUTION

Then, in 1952, there was a coup d'état by President Fulgencio Batista, and a military dictatorship was established, restricting freedom of speech. Years later, Fidel Castro and his revolutionaries began the Cuban Revolution, and my hometown of Santiago and the Oriente province became the epicenter.

I remember waking up in the middle of the night to

gunshots, and having to hide under the mattress to avoid the bullets in my home. My room was facing the street, so we needed to barricade every night. Those were similar experiences to that of my Puerto Rican patients at Brookdale Hospital Outpatient mental health clinic in Brownsville, Brooklyn, where they also had to barricade the apartment's door every night to protect themselves against the drug addicts.

I was just fifteen or sixteen, and supported the social justice principles that Castro's revolution was advocating, and I was thrilled listening to his speeches about giving every Cuban access to free education, health care, employment and housing.

The revolutionary process was traumatic, because there were days that I was leaving my home to go to school, and on the sidewalk, I saw many young men who were killed by the dictator Batista forces. That was my first encounter with the death of young people who deeply believe in social justice and wanted to do the best for their country—and they were killed because they couldn't exercise those rights. That was traumatic and left scars, because I think that people should be able to express their political concerns and advocate for the common good of society, without having to pay the price with their lives.

Then came a hard decision. I couldn't go to Villanueva University in Havana because of the political situation. I ended up going to the University of Santiago, and I got a bachelor's degree in sociology, because psychology was not being offered at that time. In a way, by looking at society and putting everything into context, I was experiencing it all as a person in my own country.

AN UNEXPECTED ROLE MODEL

It was during those first two years of Fidel Castro's administration that Elena Mederos became the first Minister of Social Services in Cuba. She emphasized the role of women and feminism in the delivery of social services. She had a position of privilege, and her whole life was dedicated to helping and understanding Cubans who lived in poverty, lacked access to health care, education, and employment.

Although Fidel came in with the concept of communism and socialism, what she added was a different perspective, and that's what made a difference in my life: the feminine perspective of poverty.

She was an early role model for me. She emphasized that women bring something special to society that has been constantly undermined and undervalued, as evidenced by the fact that women have the most difficult challenges in being poor. She believed that the world would be a better world if women were elected/appointed to lead countries. Years later I co-authored, The Maria Paradox, a book about reparation, healing, self-empowerment of Latina women, the "Nueva Marianistas" which integrates Elena Mederos world view of powerful Latinas.

I clearly remember her concept that if there's going to be fairness for women, then you must talk about women becoming leaders in different fields such as social services, academia, health, economy, and many others, because you cannot think of women having no choice other than being in the home. What she was saying is, women have to play a role beyond what's described by society, namely being a mother.

In fact, her thinking about women's place in society plays out in my career: I have been the first Latina social worker holding leadership positions such as Chairperson of the New York Health and Hospital Corporation, the largest public hospital system in the world; senior health policy advisor to the New York City Mayor; New York City Health Administrator; Executive Deputy Commissioner for Families and Children at the New York City Health Human Resources Administration; University Dean for Health Science and Vice-Chair of the Board of Directors, Federal Reserve of New York, which is one of the twelve districts of the Federal Reserve that is in charge of monetary policy in the U.S.

ARRIVING IN NEW YORK

I was terribly disappointed that freedom of speech disappeared in Cuba as the Revolution evolved. It probably wasn't what Elena Mederos would have recommended, but I felt compelled to defend liberty and freedom of speech, and got involved with some counter-revolutionary activities—and I did pay the price, going to jail for some days. It was then my father decided that it was too risky for me to be in my hometown, and he put me on a plane to New York City with only the clothes I was wearing and $5 in my pocket.

The four-hour flight was traumatic, leaving behind family and friends and a country that is tropical and warm, only to arrive in a land where all I could see from the airplane window was a blanket of white snow. Nothing green; I was in shock.

It was a cold January night, and I found out what it was like to have no boots after a twenty-inch snowfall the night before. My sister had been sent with me, and our uncle picked us up at the airport and gave us coats to wear. This was the first out of many instances that I had to go through the process of acculturation and learn new ways, not only of dressing, but changing behaviors to be more consistent with American culture. I had first-hand experience with "acculturation stress," as described in the behavioral health literature on immigrants, and that I observed in many Latinx immigrants today.

This experience makes my heart go out to Latinx immigrants today who are trying to escape political or economic hardship. The plight of the immigrant is often a Pandora's box that when you open it up, it's going to open up a lot of stuff that maybe you didn't expect. Being a Cuban refugee in 1961 was not as difficult as it is to be an immigrant in 2021.

LOOKING FOR A JOB

Once in New York, I needed to find a job. I took the first job I was offered—as a secretary. It was a challenge to get there because I had to get over my fear of the subway and being underground. In Cuba, the only time you went underground was when you were buried.

The boss at the office wanted me to type a letter. It took the whole day. He paid me $25, and we parted ways. It was an act of kindness, because he knew after an hour that I couldn't do the job.

What I have learned, and this is what I have tried to work on with my patients and in whatever position I have held, is to ask, "What do I bring to these situations? What are my strengths? What is it that I have? How can I improve the lives of others?" Because every human being has something of value.

In my introspection, I acknowledged that I knew Spanish. So, I looked for places where they needed Spanish speakers. And there it was: a radio station and magazine, looking for a receptionist who spoke English and Spanish.

When they wouldn't increase my pay to equal the work I was doing, it was time to look for another job. This time it was the International Rescue Committee who was looking for a receptionist. It's an organization that brings in refugees from all over the world, and it quickly became home—and eventually opened up other opportunities. Those led me to Catholic Charities, which was opening a center for Cuban refugees; and then to the American Council for Emigrees, and a chance to earn my master's degree.

LEARNING PROGRAM PLANNING

I earned my master's degree in social work at Fordham University and received a scholarship from Catholic Charities of Brooklyn, where I worked after I completed my master studies. I was asked to develop the adoption department. It was my first exposure to program planning.

During my master's program, I could have chosen to go into management and administration, but I didn't know that

I had the talent for that at the time. I only knew that I had a talent for interpersonal, group, and clients. I loved the exposure to management, program planning, and development.

I eventually took a job with Brookdale Hospital Community Mental Health Center, where I ran a group session for Latina mothers. The attendance was low, and I discovered it was because the time I'd chosen was the same as the soap opera, *Novela*. So, I did home visits, and decided to create the mothers' group at their home to watch it, and eventually, we were able to talk about their *own* novelas. The integration of cultural competency into social work practice requires modifications to model interventions that we have learned in our graduate programs.

This was not the only time I learned about the relevancy of understanding the patient's culture in treatment, where they may have a different understanding of health and illness, as well as help seeking behaviors that are different from the American perspective. I integrated cultural competency in my social work practice in clinical, management, and policy fields. That is a lesson for all of us social workers.

I also needed to have a thorough understanding and knowledge of the economic, health, and social policies, as well as discrimination that created the poverty that I saw in Brownsville, Brooklyn, New York and that undermined the lives of the Latinx and African American clients that I worked with. That's when I decided to get a doctorate degree in policy, planning, and administration at Adelphi University, to learn how social policies are created in the U.S., and use that knowledge as a tool to foster changes in the lives of so many underserved Latinos and other communities. I learned quickly about "incrementalism," the preferred mode for policy development in the U.S., which is quite different from a revolution as I lived in Cuba.

REFLECTION

My legacy is to bring the cultural values that I grew up with into focus, which are community, family, collaboration, and the common good—and participate in some way in changing society for the public welfare of all citizen but particularly Latinx and underserved communities. It is the opposite of individualism and competitiveness, which are the cornerstone of American society's values.

I believe that a few of my contributions to the common good include implementing health managed care; preventing the closure of the public hospital system; creating health insurance for small businesses; developing the first medical respite programs and developing supportive housing for low income and homeless chronically ill individuals; increasing economic development opportunities for the Latinx and underserved communities; contributing to developing policies for grandparents and family members to become foster parents; creating a successful Latinx community based organization, Comunilife, Inc; establishing the Multicultural Relational Approach Model and developing a Latinx community-defined program to reduce suicide among Latina adolescents in New York City, with the goal of becoming an evidenced based practice.

For me, social work is a unique, practice-based profession and academic to promote social change, social cohesion and the empowerment and liberation of people. Thus, it is a call to action to change the social reality of the Latinx community today. We can play a critical role in changing the disparities in social welfare, health, mental health, and the economic well-being of "nuestra gente." I encourage social workers to read Paulo Freire influential work, Pedagogy of the Oppressed, which is considered one of the foundation text of the critical pedagogy movement.

ABOUT THE AUTHOR

Dr. Rosa M. Gil, Comunilife's Founder, President, and CEO, has had a distinguished career in New York City's health, mental health, supportive housing, social service, and higher education sectors. Since Comunilife opened in 1989, she has centered the work on the intersection between health and housing, with the goal of addressing the critical social determinants of health and enhancing the health outcomes of New York City's underserved communities.

Under Dr. Gil's stewardship, Comunilife has developed more than 2,678 units of affordable and supportive housing for the city's hardest to reach residents, the homeless, mentally ill, and people living with HIV/AIDS and other health conditions. Under her leadership, Comunilife created *Life is Precious*™, *a nationally recognized program for Latina teen at risk of suicide and also created the New York City's premiere Medical Respite Program.*

Dr. Gil has recently been appointed to the NYS Vaccine Equity Task Force, as well as numerous other federal, state, and city commissions and boards, including the Federal Reserve Bank of New York (deputy chair), The NYS Suicide Prevention Council, The Board of Health (NYC Department of Health and Mental Hygiene), NYS Governor's Interagency Council on Homelessness, The Commission of Health Care Facilities in the 21st Century (The Berger Commission), and the Minority Women Panel on Health Experts (U.S. Public Health Services). Dr. Gil is a member of the President Carter Mental Health Task Force and the Board of Trustees of EmblemHealth.

Dr. Rosa Gil is one of the founders of the Urban Institute for Behavioral Health of New York City, Latino Commission on AIDS, the Association of Hispanic Mental Health Professionals, and 100 Hispanic Women. She has published numerous articles on mental health, ethnicity, child welfare, and gender issues. She is the co-author of the Maria Paradox, the first authoritative book on self-esteem and Hispanic women.

Dr. Rosa M. Gil, DSW
FB: @comunilifeinc
IG: @comunilife
Twitter: @drrosagil

Madrina

MY MIGRATION STORY: HOPE AND THE CYCLE OF HEALING

ROSA MARIA BRAMBLE CABALLERO, LCSW-R

"For asylum seekers the struggle is forced migration: "there is a part of me that doesn't want to be here" because of all that is left behind due to persecution."

EL VIAJE: LOSS AND GRIEF

My family struggled in their journey to the United States. My mother owned a restaurant in Caracas, Venezuela. When she made the difficult decision to come to the U.S., she left it all behind. My father, an electrician, was already in New York.

Consistent with Latinx culture, she followed the principle, "Seguir al esposo." We had been comfortable, lived well, and were surrounded by uncles and aunts who would gather on Sundays and eat *pabellon,* our national dish of rice, beans, shredded beef, and plantains. I remember feeling such a sense of community and home. But we had to leave. My father was concerned about the political instability and school disruption taking place in Venezuela.

The sudden change affected our family, especially my mother, who lost not only her economic stability, but all of what is familiar to her, especially her language. The first years were traumatic for our family. My mother used all of the earnings from her restaurant as a down payment for a house in Brooklyn, New York. My parents fell prey to scam realtors and attorneys, and her $12,000 evaporated. While living in a rented room, our jewelry was stolen. We had nothing except each other.

The losses and trauma of migration left my mother vulnerable to depression, which she suffered for the rest of the time she lived in New York. Her family was originally from Colombia, and she had migrated to Venezuela as a little girl, where she experienced discrimination. Migrating to the U.S. forced her to relive the displacement and sense of alienation that immigrants often experience.

While we developed a network of friends, the stress was palpable. In my family, the stress of migration, loss of extended family, and adjusting to the new culture set us apart. The stressors especially affected my brother, Antonio, who suffered from mental illness. Tonito, as we dearly called him, passed away due to mental illness when he was nineteen. My brother Alvaro eventually returned to Venezuela due to the trauma of racial profiling and racism he experienced as a Black young adult male in the U.S. He feared that he would get killed by the police because of the color of his skin. The tension between my parents increased, and it eventually led to my parents' separation. When my father left the home, my mother gave up completely. She gave up hope.

THE GOOD GIRL

One evening in October, when I was fourteen, my mother announced that she was returning to Venezuela. As she packed her suitcase, she added, "And I'm not coming back." Suddenly, I felt very unsafe, alone, and abandoned. The fear of abandonment became a theme in my life for many years, and shaped later relational decisions.

Had anyone called Child Protective Services, my two brothers and I would have probably been separated. I'm not sure what my life would have been should that have occurred. Having been raised in a very overprotective environment and then suddenly not having parents gave me freedom way beyond what is normal for that age. I would go off with my friends, miss school, and go out with the "cool" guys. I was extremely naïve about being street smart.

One day, I hung out with a crowd of school friends in an empty apartment in Queens. The police were called, and we were taken to family court, charged with trespassing. In my naivete, I had no idea what was happening. We were taken in front of a judge, who sent a couple of the girls to group homes. When it was my turn, he looked at me and said, "You shouldn't be here... I'm giving you this chance to go home because you're a good girl, and you're just hanging out with the wrong crowd. I'm going to let you go." I sometimes wonder if the judge was able to see that my behavior was a way to connect and belong, and that it wasn't my true self. What would have happened if I was sent to a group home and experienced the trauma of further familial fragmentation? I'm sure that my life would have taken a very different path. This experience began to shape my life.

At that time, at the age of fifteen, my brothers and sister felt that I needed to be with my mother for supervision and guidance. I was sent to live with my mother in Venezuela where, over time, she had built a new home and opened a small restaurant, "El Doral." I was happy to be with my mother, and I admired her perseverance in starting her life again. Although there were challenging family dynamics, going back to Venezuela was an edifying experience. I was re-connected with my country, culture, extended family and friends, and salsa music! Music and dance are integral to my life, and songs like "Canta Y Se Quita Tu Dolor," "La Vida es un Carnaval," and "Lloraras" just run through my veins!

For a few years of my life, I lived and worked in Venezuela and sometimes returned to the visit the U.S., living in two worlds, holding two realities. As do many immigrants, I live with the experience of where I belong. In Venezuela, people say that I dress differently now and my mannerisms are different. In the United States, my Black race is centered as my only identity. I may have a slight accent at times, but it's inevitable that I get the question, "But where are you really from?" I am often told, "You don't look Venezuelan." I began the journey of my bicultural and bilingual experience, using this privilege to embrace diversity, and to connect with communities of color and immigrants.

LEGACY OF RESILIENCE: THE CALL TO SOCIAL WORK

Unfortunately, my education was neglected in Venezuela during the critical years of high school. I eventually returned to New York, where I obtained a GED, attended a community college, and then transferred to Hunter College of the City of New York, where I received my bachelor's degree.

By this time, my father was back in my life and our relationship grew to be very close. I always refer to him as my spiritual guide; he taught me to be humble, to be nonjudgmental, and to connect to others with respect.

I came to realize that I had the power to make decisions to change my life and the lives of others. The power to act, to give voice to injustice, and to organize began to emerge. My mother was a great storyteller, and when she told me more about my maternal grandmother, "Mama Rosa," a lot came together for me. My grandmother was born in Colombia in the early 1900s. A beautiful Black woman with high cheekbones, she came together with my grandfather, who was a white Spaniard. Their relationship was not the norm and was not accepted; they were products of colonialism and a racist society at the time.

She responded to the impoverished conditions of marginalized communities. She gathered food and extra clothing which she gave to those in need—she was a community organizer at heart! Over the course of my career, community service, perseverance, of acting began to take shape and weave into the legacy of resiliency shaped by my grandmother and my ancestors.

My journey as a social worker began while working as a case manager at a home daycare center, where the program director, Flo Ceravalo, and my immediate supervisor, Robin Williams, both licensed clinical social workers, encouraged me to consider graduate school. My supervisor took me to a nearby ACS (Agency of Children Services) prevention center, where social workers provide therapeutic interventions with families to prevent further child abuse and neglect. She explained that with a social work degree, I could help families in that capacity. She told me, "You can do it. You can make it happen."

THE UNTAPPED LEADER WITHIN ME

My degree in social work gave me the tools to address the unmet needs of our communities. Challenging myself to the next level allowed me to connect with the untapped leader part within me. In 1998, I worked for the Child Center of New York in Queens, a borough that is considered the most diverse place in the nation, maybe the world. One day I read an internal agency posting looking for project director to oversee a program to meet the mental health needs of women and children living with HIV. Although I had no previous experience in program development, grant writing, or community linkages, I felt the need to serve at a macro level, addressing the inequity in healthcare access in marginalized and vulnerable communities. I took the risk.

Developing a program, hiring staff, supervision, building community linkages, writing monthly reports, and attending community meetings were all new and challenging to me. The team spirit was crucial in providing mental health services to clients who suffered trauma, depression, anxiety, and family rejection due to HIV. While gratifying, the work also brought along the heaviness of grief, loss, and community healing. I began to appreciate the importance of self-care in our profession, although I admit that at times it took an emotional toll.

In 2002, I coordinated the first community forum to address the impact of HIV on Latinas titled, "Soy Latina Soy Positva." This forum brought together community members and epidemiologists from Elmhurst Hospital to discuss barriers to treatment and to bring visibility to issues such mental health, housing, and the stigma surrounding HIV.

My mantra became "My passion makes action." It was in that light that I became the co-founder of Voces Latinas, an organization dedicated to the prevention of HIV and violence in the Latinx community. I had already developed a strong community reputation, and I was therefore able to gain support for the organization. My HIV seropositive Latina clients who established a deep *confianza* in me supported the organization by becoming board members and giving testimony in the spirit of awareness, prevention, and advocacy. I brought the informal psychoeducational format used in alcohol prevention to create a structured intervention and framework that bridged the gap in services especially since the rates of HIV among women of color was increasing at an alarming rate.

THE ENTREPRENEUR

After working many years in outpatient agency-based practice, I gradually began my private practice in 2006. When the federal grant for the mental health program was not renewed in 2008, I had to make the choice to either continue agency practice or to dive into full-time private practice. This decision was difficult, but I decided with the confidence that my private practice would grow. I vividly recalled the first day after signing the commercial lease contract. I panicked and thought, "What did I do, I can't make this happen."

Having a niche is key to success, because you build an expertise and are sought out. I started writing immigration forensic psychosocial evaluations when an immigration attorney from a community legal service clinic asked me to serve as a translator. After gaining some experience in interviewing clients and writing reports for the clinic, I sought to deepen my skills in writing these reports. I took trainings offered by the Physicians for Human Rights Asylum Project, where I am now an evaluator.

I am often asked as to why I focused on this type of work, which is exhaustive in bearing witness to multiple traumatic stories. Themes of childhood abuse, intimate partner violence, the trauma of poverty, and family dysfunction are frequently reported. It still brings tears to my eyes in thinking of an adult Latino male who cried, "Solo queria un caminocito para jugar." As therapists, we value the spiritual dimensions of healing and post traumatic growth. The Internal Family Systems compassionate framework in trauma recovery gives me the language to give let the client know they can give themselves permission to heal transgenerational trauma, legacy, and cultural burdens. When we unburden parts holding pain, shame, and negative beliefs, it frees up energy to restore trust in Self and Self-Led Leadership. This approach has been transformative for my clients and in my own personal and professional life.

REFLECTION

I have embraced the cycle of healing. As we bear witness and work to heal others, we are also healing the wounded parts of ourselves. My mother had a history of trauma and as a result, she was not always available to me. Without any intervention, the impact of trauma persisted intergenerationally. My mother passed away in September 2016. When we caravanned by our home and her restaurant, I cried in honoring how much of a survivor she was, all the lives that she touched, and her spirit of life. She did her best with the options she had. I invoke her entrepreneurial spirit, "la emprendedora," with the ebbs and flows as a business owner. I can also cherish the time we had together and our love for each other.

The journey of healing restores hope, and for immigrants, the power of community healing restores dreams, and opens opportunities and healthy connections, for themselves, their children, and for generations to come.

ABOUT THE AUTHOR

Rosa Maria Bramble Caballero is a bilingual licensed clinical social worker who serves as founder and president of Caballero Counseling and Consulting Services. With over fifteen years of clinical experience, Rosa has specialized in the psychosocial assessment and trauma-informed treatment of immigrant populations.

She earned her master's degree in social work from Hunter College and has completed post graduate training in family therapy, advanced trauma studies, Sensorimotor Psychotherapy, and Internal Family Systems, where she is a currently a member of the IFS Diversity and Inclusion Committee, the Advanced Training Program with the goal to bring the model to the Latinx community. Rosa conducts forensic biopsychosocial evaluations for asylum and immigration cases, and she provides expert testimony on trauma and impact of deportation on children and families. She is frequently sought after for consultation and collaboration in legal and advocacy services, maternal health, gender-based violence, unaccompanied minors, and trauma-informed care.

Rosa served as the president of the New York City Chapter of the National Association of Puerto Rican and Hispanic Social Workers (NAPRHSW), and she was appointed to the New York City HIV Planning Council (2002-2004) by the Office of Mayor Michael Bloomberg. Rosa is an adjunct lecturer at Columbia University School of Social Work, where she teaches several advanced clinical and practical courses, including a course on trauma-informed treatment for asylum seekers and immigrants. She also serves as board member of the Project ICI participatory community research board at Columbia University and the University of Michigan, where she helps study collaboration among HIV service providers. She founded the Venezuelan Community Support Center, Inc., to address the needs of Venezuelan refugees and Latinx survivors of trauma at all stages of migration. Rosa is frequently invited to speak and facilitate workshops at academic institutions as well as national and international conferences. She recently was a guest at the Jorge Ramos special coverage of the 20th Remembrance of 9/11, where she discussed her advocacy for the undocumented workers of Ground Zero. She has several peer-reviewed publications spanning language interpretation, trauma-informed care, HIV, program development, community violence intervention, vicarious trauma, and resilience.

Rosa has been awarded numerous honors, including the Union Square Award and the Latino Social Work Taskforce Community Service Award. She is the proud mother of two amazing adult children, Jacqueline and John, who bring joy, inspiration, and life lessons. She enjoys music, working out, travel, dance, cooking, and spending time with her family and friends.

EDUCATION WAS MY CONSTANT

JESSICA HARDIAL, LCSW, MA

THE MUDDY SURROUNDINGS

Growing up in a Latinx household, I witnessed and felt many things. They mentioned to me often how in their countries, education was not a priority. My parents hoped I would finish high school, however, they expected me to be a teenage mother and drop out of school. Both of my parents instilled values in me that revolved around being a mother and wife.

My mother was born and raised in the Dominican Republic. She dropped out of school in the fifth grade because her parents couldn't afford for her to continue her studies. My father was born and raised in Ecuador. He dropped out of school in the sixth grade to help his father work to maintain his family. As a boy, he was taught men take care of their families.

From a very young age, my mother defined the roles for my brother and me. My brother didn't help around the house because he would have a wife to do that. For me, she taught me how to cook, clean, and maintain a household from the age of six. She didn't care much about my educational studies because she wanted to prepare me for "real life" as a wife and mother.

My father was physically, emotionally, and mentally abusive toward my mother and me. He came from a background where men ruled the home and women were in place to serve their husbands. My father was a machoistic man and was always in charge.

I remember the first time I witnessed my father hit my mother. I was five, and I still remember it. We were getting the car ready to head to the park. My mother forgot to bring the ice. He became so angry with her. He yelled at her and then punched her in the ear. I remember the blood running down her face. She didn't say anything. I was so scared.

As the years progressed, my father became more aggressive and possessive over my mother. She wasn't allowed to have male friends or wear makeup or hang out with her sisters unless he authorized it. The number of times I witnessed domestic violence in my home became immeasurable. My family and I quickly became acquainted with the 102nd Precinct, due to many calls made for domestic violence.

I cannot remember when my loving father, the man I looked up to, the man I ran to greet at the door as I heard the keys turn the lock, the man who made me feel like a princess, the man who lovingly called me "Chikita," turned into a man who beat me so hard I felt worthless.

My innocence was stripped from me so suddenly with no warning, no explanation. Just tears and emptiness. I remember that morning like if it was yesterday. I was sick and my mother let me stay home from school. I was lying in bed when my father called me into the kitchen to go get his slippers from the other room. I went to get up, but my mother told me to go back to bed. He continued to yell for me, but I ignored him and eventually fell asleep. The next morning when I woke up, my father wasn't talking to me. I knew he was angry. I wanted more than anything to be out of the house. I rushed into the shower, but I was too late. My father stopped me in front of the bathroom door. He instructed me to lay flat on the towel on the floor. I was so scared. I shut my eyes tight, clenched my body, and before the cable wire hit my back, I began to tremble. I don't remember if it was the fear or the pain from the whipping that brought me to tears. My mother ran up the stairs to stop him and he turned his anger toward her. I remember lying on my bed in my room crying while I heard her scream for him to stop beating her. He finally stopped and left for work.

I became a shy, timid child who suffered in silence. No one noticed the physical abuse I endured, which elevated my feelings of not being good enough to be noticed. With feelings of not being good enough, I strived to be the quiet, overachieving student in school. I worked hard in school to gain my father's approval. Deep down, I wanted to feel good enough for him to be proud of.

I had multiple realities within my childhood. My friendships along with school became my escape from my home reality. I quickly realized that education became my constant form of happiness. I felt fulfilled at school away from my father, who caused me so much pain. At home, I had to face the reality of my father's abuse toward my mother and me. I learned and utilized techniques to shield myself from falling into despair. I self-soothed during arguments and violent episodes in my childhood home. I learned how to control my emotions during my episodes of feeling inadequate.

Throughout the abuse my mother and I experienced, he made me feel that women weren't smart enough or pretty enough, and we were useless.

I remember being in elementary school and studying really hard for my weekly tests. All of my tests needed to be signed by a parent or guardian to acknowledge student progress. I remember the first time I scored a 98 on my exam. I was proud of achieving a high score and couldn't wait to show my parents. As I walked in the house, I immediately showed my father. He refused to sign it. He yelled at me, ridiculed me, and called me stupid for not achieving a perfect score. I was traumatized and my excitement quickly turned to disappointment.

My determination to gain approval from him elevated. My father had very high expectations of me. He instilled my need to always achieve a 100 on every exam. For every test, if received anything other than a 100, I experienced anger and sadness within myself and I internalized. I developed low self-esteem. To this day, I am a terrible test taker. Because of this, I've always felt like an imposter throughout my social work career. It took many years to process the trauma I experienced. The anxiety and fear of taking exams always brings me back to my childhood trauma.

THE LOTUS FLOWER

I faced many challenges while pursuing my social work career. My main challenge was money. I didn't have the privilege that others had. In high school, I worked to pay for my graduation dues and prom because my parents couldn't afford it. My father refused to come to my high school graduation, and my mother couldn't attend because she got denied a personal day. She worked three jobs to sustain the household expenses. It was a bittersweet moment when I graduated because my mother could not be there. I was proud of myself, but did not know how to celebrate myself. I knew this was just the beginning of more financial barriers. The social stressors were prevalent, simultaneously I was experiencing the aftermath of coming out to my parents.

As a proud member of the LGBTQIA+ community, I came out to my family at the age of fifteen. After graduating from high school, I was displaced because my father didn't approve of my sexual orientation.

My biggest challenge was finding an apartment, working forty-six hours a week while attending college full-time. I did not qualify for financial aid due to my father claiming me as a dependent and refusing to give me his tax information. I cried in the financial aid office. It was a difficult time for me, and I wasn't sure if education and my career goals were worth the fight. I felt defeated and had a 1.75 GPA. I received 2 F grades, 1 WU grade and 1 D- grade.

I wanted to drop out and felt school wasn't for me. I ruminated, lost sleep, and coped by performing to reduce my anxiety. Determined, I turned on my computer and registered for classes though I was working full-time to survive. Post graduating with my Associate's from BMCC, I transferred to Queens College, and I majored in psychology. This was the beginning to my social work journey.

At my first job as a foster care caseworker right after graduating with my bachelor's degree, I was one of five Latinx community members in that work environment. I recall advocating for a child who spoke Spanish on my caseload. My client refused to have parent-child visits with her mother, and I supported her needs. Her mother was angry and called a meeting with the supervisor, director, and parent advocate to request a new caseworker. The director of the program simply stated, "I do not have any other Spanish-speaking caseworkers, because many don't have college degrees, since they drop out of high school to have a bunch of kids." I recall feeling shocked and powerless. Everyone was quiet, but her macroaggression was loud. I have replayed that meeting in my mind countless times, reflecting on what I should have said, could have said, but didn't.

As a proud educated adult of immigrants who identifies as a Latina, I have encountered multiple microaggressions and felt discriminated in different work environments. Imposter syndrome became a real challenge for me during these times. I would break down and cry, and feel as if I was not good enough. I would isolate myself for days and would stay quiet to rejuvenate. I learned to believe in myself and acknowledge my hard work. I became my own advocate. I know my purpose, and it is to inspire others to believe in themselves despite the thorns that pricked them. I may not feel like the smartest person in the room all the time, but I know I am the most determined. I am still a work in progress, a blossoming lotus.

BLOSSOMING LOTUS

I have made multiple investments in my life. I invested in healing, learning, living. I loved openly with pride, and though freedom was expensive, it is priceless for me. My education was the key to my success, and though fearful of test taking, I made an investment in myself and continued the path to become credentialed. One of the largest emotional investments I made was registering for my social work exams. The financial investment and the time to accumulate hours was exhausting. The process of applying was not easy; the forms, the fees, and the verified experience all provoked anxiety before taking the actual exam.

After my financial investment, I was proud to PASS and obtain my Licensed Master Social Worker (LMSW) certification during the first attempt. The Licensed Clinical Social Worker (LCSW) exam was very challenging, especially since it was during a global pandemic. After multiple attempts and feeling unmotivated, anxious, fearful, and traumatized, the emotional investment was worth it. I passed and became a business owner who is now pursuing a doctoral degree.

I am a first-generation high school graduate. I am the first Latina in my family to complete my bachelor's degree, my master's degree and currently pursuing my doctorate degree. Being a Latina has shaped me both personally and professionally in many ways. It has impacted me personally due to the many social constructs of what my role as a woman should be. I challenged the norms of our culture within my family.

I remember my nine-year-old niece, Sarah, saying, "I want to be like you and pursue college to help people." I felt so much pride as I now serve as a role model. It is possible. I honor my mother's sacrifices with every degree that I've obtained. My nieces admire who I am as a woman, as a Latina and as a social worker. Although we come from a culture where young women don't prioritize education, I have redirected and paved the path for the next generation. I am planting the seeds to many future blossoming lotus flowers.

I believe every Latina has a motive as to why they strive to succeed. My motive was to heal from my childhood traumas and help my mother move forward. I owe my success to my mother, Maria. I admire her strength and courage in migrating to this country and overcoming the obstacles of intimate partner violence. Mami's resilience and determination became my own qualities. Our interconnected generational trauma also helped us to be resilient forces of nature.

As a clinical social worker, I practice with the core values of integrity, service, and competence through a social justice lens, and the importance of human relationships. The dignity and worth of a person are some of the most important core values to practice through. Through my personal journey, I understand the significance of using the strengths-based perspective of each individual to help them succeed. In my practice, I recognize my privilege and position of power and use it to advocate and not harm, as society has already caused great oppression.

Through my childhood traumas and feeling powerless, I learned how to navigate and heal. This allowed me to understand my purpose to support children and adolescents who also feel powerless. I support adolescents with their feelings of loneliness, anxiety, depression, despair, and isolation. I help families and adolescents communicate to support the healing process without judgment through a trauma-informed lens. My own personal struggles allow me to understand the dynamics of family work.

What I am most proud of is my humility. My mother always taught me no matter how successful or well-off I become, to always remember where I came from and to give back to my community. I give back through teaching and guiding students as an undergraduate lecturer at a college and as a SIFI instructor. Despite my many challenges, I made it! I would like to see more beautiful Latinas make it too, and I hope my story inspires you to not give up.

REFLECTION

Social work is very important today because of what social work stands for: working on improving the lives of others. I didn't choose social work; it chose me. From a young age, I knew I wanted to make a difference in the world but didn't know how. It took some time to truly understand my purpose in life. I want you to reflect on:

- What drew you to the social work field?
- What is your motive?
- What is your purpose?

Once you can answer that, you will be able to fulfil your purpose. There will be many obstacles in your way, but keep true to your purpose and you will move past the obstacles. Remember the why and you will succeed.

ABOUT THE AUTHOR

Jessica Hardial is a bilingual clinical social worker who has over ten years of social work experience. She received her associates degree in liberal arts from CUNY Borough of Manhattan Community College in 2011, then her bachelor's degree in psychology and sociology with a minor in student services and counseling from CUNY Queens College in 2013. Shortly after, she received her master's degree in social work from Fordham University in 2016. Jessica completed her second master's degree in human development from Fielding Graduate University in 2021.

Jessica Hardial is a School Social Worker for the NYC Department of Education, serves as an adjunct lecturer for SUNY Old Westbury, and is currently a Ph.D. student attending Fielding Graduate University. Jessica has a private practice, Blossoming Lotus Therapy, LCSW PLLC, where she specializes in working with children, adolescents, young adults, and families.

She is passionate about working with LGBTQIA+ community members and their families, the foster care and adoption population, and children of immigrants. Jessica specializes in issues surrounding trauma, anxiety, and family conflict using a somatic oriented approach. Jessica continues to enhance the social work profession by providing supervision to graduate students and post graduate students to enhance their clinical skills in their field of practice.

Jessica Hardial

jessicahardiallcsw@gmail.com

FB & IG:

@Jessicahardiallcsw

@Blossominglotustherapy

PAIN'S BLESSINGS

MARIA E. ORTIZ, M.A., LMSW

I was told, more than once, that I should write my story. I would quietly think, "Me? I don't have much to write about, especially compared to the stories I hear!" It was more likely I would repeat the cycle of poverty given the life I had as a child. I was not expected to earn two master's degrees, become a licensed social worker, live in a luxury building in the same neighborhood I grew up in, and sit as a member of Manhattan Community Board 4 as co-chair of the Housing, Health, and Human Services committee. Community Board 4 represents the neighborhood where I was raised, Chelsea and Hell's Kitchen.

ACTS OF SERVICE

My mother, brother, and I lived in Hell's Kitchen on 50th Street between 10th and 11th Avenue in a walkup on the second level, where the hallway to get to the one-bedroom apartment was extremely narrow. The bathtub was in the kitchen, by a window that faced our neighbor. The bathroom had no sink but did have an old-fashioned high tank pull-chain toilet. The landlord was forgiving and empathetic; he understood my mother could not afford to pay the rent every month.

When you live in poverty, you cannot afford basic things like toilet paper or toothpaste, and sometimes we had to go without. There are also times you do not have enough food to eat—but one way to get more food was to volunteer at a food pantry. So, we did, often. We would volunteer at two churches in the community bagging food and sometimes stayed to help give them out. Though we did not have much, there were things we could do to help others.

After earning my bachelor's degree, I applied to work at Rheedlan Place, a nonprofit with offices in Hell's Kitchen. Today, they are known as the Harlem Children's Zone and no longer have offices in Midtown. As a child, our family received their help. I was happy to have a social worker come to our home to lead "family meetings," listen to me, and a safe place to go to in the community that my mother trusted. Helping others remained with me. It fed my soul and I felt a need to help families in my own community. I felt the deepest amount of joy when I would volunteer at a family shelter with young children in Midtown near the entrance to the Lincoln Tunnel.

Work for my community did not end there. My community includes where my son attends school. I volunteer at almost every school he attends, being part of some parent group. Serving others helps in a way you may never learn. I have been fortunate to occasionally hear how my innate desire to help has impacted others.

BEING A WOMAN OF COLOR

As I have become older and come into positions of leadership, I see I am not surrounded by many women or people of color. The exception has been when I became part of the NASW NYC Chapter.

In 2014, I became part of Community Board 4. After a short time, I considered leaving. Attending three meetings a month was burdensome with a young son in tow, but something kept me committed. Part of it was my desire to contribute to my community, partially because I felt a sense of obligation. Out of fifty people, I was one of about ten women and there were less than five people of color. Also, many members lived in the community for a short time and were making decisions about the community where I was born and raised, and raising my son in. I thought it was important I stay involved. My voice needed to be heard too.

While on the Community Board, I added to my plate. I joined my son's elementary school's Parent Teacher Association and the local hospital's advisory board. In both groups, there were not many people of color. I also noticed this pattern when I worked for the City of New York. The people in positions of leadership lacked diversity.

Being raised in New York City in Midtown Manhattan in

the eighties meant there was a lot of ethnic diversity and most families were lower or middle-income levels. Our family however, struggled with poverty. Regardless, I had teachers that believed in me. I did have one teacher that was extremely giving and kind to our family in many ways, but as I became an adult, I realized that she did not see the full potential in me.

While I was in high school, this teacher suggested I could become an airline stewardess. At the time, I thought it was a good idea although I was not interested in that career. I was interested in science, psychology, and abnormal psychology, but this teacher never suggested becoming more than an airline stewardess. I believe part of this was because I am Latina and the home I came from: a Latina-led single-parent household with a mother in recovery from alcohol abuse, struggling with depression, living in poverty.

UNINTENDED CONSEQUENCES

The trauma of poverty impacted my sense of self-worth. People in my life who I deeply valued were not able to picture me living well and becoming a career professional. Undoubtedly, my sense of self was also impacted by my father's choice not to be involved, by being molested, and by my mother's personal struggles. How could I see my own worth when many around me did not, even if indirectly?

I was offered a case manager position at Rheedlan Place after I expressed interest in working there. I declined the offer. I felt unprepared. How could I possibly do that job?! I was more comfortable being with children, so I worked in the after-school program instead. Similarly, after some time working in child welfare at the NYC Administration for Children's Services, I could have applied to be a supervisor, but did not. The fear crept in again. I had the time, knowledge, and a graduate degree, but used my son as the excuse not to apply. How could I possibly be "good enough" to be a supervisor? These feelings also rose to the surface when I applied for different positions and was not offered a role. Negative self-talk happens. We all experience it.

I also experienced a period when all of the volunteering was taking a toll. I did not know how to say no. I felt obligated to do and to give of my time. I felt exhausted. It also felt exhausting to be one of few people of color in many spaces. I felt the responsibility to have to speak for women, or Latinx, or single parents.

IT TAKES A VILLAGE

My life was most stable when my mother was receiving help from others. When I was younger than ten years old, she attended Alcoholics Anonymous (AA) and was part of a day treatment program where she also received counseling to address coping with depression. I have pictures of me about three or four years old, attending AA with her. I recall it being fun; I was the only child present, so I would get snacks and lots of positive adult attention.

My mother was abstinent from alcohol for about ten years and in that time struggled on and off with depression. My grandmother and maternal side of the family stepped up to help during these times. I remember being with my brother at my grandmother's place in the projects in Chelsea or being in the Bronx at my relative's house in Castle Hill. I even recall being about ten or twelve years old and running away from home to my family's house in the Bronx. Of course, they called my mother right away and I had to go back home the next day. Nonetheless, these times were good memories for me.

We also had Buelah, the next-door neighbor we could see from our kitchen bathtub into her kitchen, who sometimes gave us things. I have an Easter picture where I look so happy wearing a new Easter dress—one that she bought for me. At this time, I attended Sacred Heart School and had two teachers there that helped our family with tangible things, provided my mother a listening ear, and support around getting us to school where my brother and I attended on a scholarship.

Part of the Sacred Heart facility space was Rheedlan Place. We had a licensed social worker from Rheedlan who would make home visits. We also would go to their afterschool program and Saturday program. What I remember most were the "family meetings." We would all sit around together, including our social worker Ellen (or case worker, Ed), and talk about any issues, good or bad. Even after we stopped working with Rheedlan when I was about ten, family meetings continued until I moved out at twenty-one years old.

Before moving out, when I was a teenager, there were many unhappy times. Painful memories of my mother being drunk, making poor choices, or not coming home, and therefore not being able to parent my younger sister and I. At this point, my brother was fortunate enough to be attending Milton Hershey School (a boarding school) working towards becoming valedictorian and attending an Ivy League University on a full scholarship. He had wonderful house parents who understood our situation. In NYC, I do not recall having anyone to rely on in the same way, but I had good people in my life who I could vent to and could sometimes spend time with—friends and relatives. They were my saving grace.

REFLECTIONS

As long as I live, I will reflect. To me, it means a way towards growth and understanding. My mother did the best she could as a single parent, but her own trauma impacted her way of parenting, thinking, perceiving, and her choices. Her traumas also impacted how she coped. Like many women who experienced her trauma, which is not my story to tell, she coped by drinking alcohol to escape from experiencing emotional pain, depression, and anxiety.

I attribute the stability we *did* experience in our lives to the support we received, whether emotional, financial, or educational, namely from social workers and the others who helped our family. My mother being open to receive help from friends, family, the church, and therapists, allowed us to see it as normal. We also viewed helping others as a normal part of growing up. Despite the hardships of growing up, I believe my mother did well in raising her three children who are compassionate, kind adults who broke many cycles in our family.

MY PURPOSE

Acts of service are one of my love languages. I often say there are pros and cons to everything, so I had to consider the con of helping others. I recognized my drive to remain in certain spaces was because I felt a need to speak for others like me. This overdeveloped sense of responsibility was also part of this. Regardless, the theme of my life has been to serve others. I have a master's in forensic psychology, but when I was getting my master's in social work, I felt I found my home, my purpose.

My "purpose" has sometimes been drowned out by other things, including my own negative self-talk. Combatting this I think will be a lifelong journey, but you can learn skills to cope with them. One for me has been to surround myself with cheerleaders, with people who can see my worth and potential, sometimes before I saw it myself. It is a blessing to have people in your life who lift you up and are not intimidated by your growth. I have been blessed to have many—even those who have been in my life for a short time.

My mother was my first cheerleader. She would say to my younger brother and I, "You are both going to have better than this, you will not live in the projects." She told us we would go on to college, graduate, and end the cycle of poverty. My mother also said she wanted me to work with women and children, but that is not what I desired to do. However, most of my life I have worked with children and families.

My passion is working with families and community work, but an important part of my purpose is parenting. I am raising my son to be a good man, a responsible man, and a man who honors and respects women. My son is my legacy. My son has had to attend many board meetings with me and has observed me help others professionally and personally. I hope my son continues this pattern of helping others.

REFLECTION

Writing this was not easy. Reminiscing about things that cause sadness, anger, or pain is hard. But it also helps with the process of healing, which takes time. Therapy helps with this process, and helps you to understand yourself better, if you are open to it. Through therapy and others in my life, I have learned to have deep compassion for myself the way I have it for others. I have learned I am worth more than I realize.

The six core values of social work are service, social justice, importance of human relationships, dignity and worth of a person, integrity and competence. Do they resonate with you? Are you curious about others, in a deep way? Are you empathetic, a good listener, do you practice self-reflection? Are you interested in learning, continually? If you answered yes to all of these, Social Work may be for you!

Two important people to know: Dr. Brene Brown and Dr. Kristin Neff.

ABOUT THE AUTHOR

As a dedicated NYC licensed social worker, Maria has a deep passion for working with families, particularly women and children. Maria has a master's degrees in forensic psychology from John Jay College and social work from Fordham University, and fifteen years of child welfare experience, in addition to over ten years of experience with children in other settings.

Currently, Maria is a forensic social worker at The Legal Aid Society in Juvenile Rights. This allows her to combine her experiences and both her graduate degrees to better engage, educate, and empower the children and youth she works with. Maria will soon transition and begin working towards becoming a licensed clinical social worker. Maria intends to provide individual therapy with a focus on serving families, especially through dyadic treatment which is where the parent and young child are treated simultaneously.

Maria serves on the board of the NASW NYC Chapter and as a Delegate Assembly member. Maria also serves on Manhattan Community Board 4 as co-chair of the Housing, Health, and Human Services Committee and serves on Arts, Culture, Education and Street Life (ACES). MCB4 covers Hell's Kitchen/Clinton, Hudson Yards, and Chelsea.

Maria continues to live in Hell's Kitchen with her son. One of her favorite hobbies to relieve stress and for self-care is to dance, especially to salsa music. During 2020, she was featured in this fun article in the "W42ST magazine."

DR. CINDY BAUTISTA-THOMAS, PH.D., LCSW, RYT

LAYING THE FOUNDATION

Rest, joy, and fun are the secrets to success, especially as a Black Latinx social worker. I was born and raised in the Highbridge section of the Bronx, in New York City. I was raised by two immigrant parents from the Dominican Republic with each having no more than a third-grade education. They taught me radical self-care. They taught me the power of rest, joy and fun. I attribute those very important lessons to the success I have experienced in my personal and professional life. I am grateful that throughout my life and all of the challenges that I encountered along the way, I have been able to center rest, joy and fun.

I grew up in the New York City Housing Authority, during the Crack Epidemic in the 1980s and 1990s. Drugs, gang violence, teenage pregnancy and poverty surrounded my community. My father was a livery cab driver and my mother was a homemaker with an entrepreneurial spirit. Our family was on public assistance and the food stamp and cash benefits we received were not enough to feed and clothe five children. My mother transformed my brother's room into a retail store, where she sold bed sheets, comforters, towels and clothing to subsidize the family's income.

Although my father struggled with alcoholism, my mother's perseverance and spiritual foundation became the impetus for each of our trajectories. We celebrated birthdays with festive parties where family members ate and danced all night long. We went to the local Catholic Church every Sunday as a family.

My mother was masterful at networking and building relationships within her neighborhood and beyond. She made sure we were active by enrolling us in church prayer groups, youth groups, after school programs, and summer enrichment programs that nurtured leadership. My mom made it look easy but we know she worked hard to manage the household while raising her children in a struggling neighborhood and my father's alcoholism. The way she shared generously of her resources, love and attention inspired me to want to do the same.

In our home, we worked hard. Rest, joy, and fun was just as essential. During the summer, we took frequent trips to the beach and the local parks to have fun and experience rest. My parents exuded joy by the way they shared family stories and shared their love with friends and family.

When financially possible, my parents took turns taking one of us to the Dominican Republic with extreme sacrifice. Our home was the hub for our childhood friends and family members. My mother was also the matriarch of her family, the eldest female of 11 siblings and that meant that our home was the landing place for my uncles and aunts that immigrated to the United States from the Dominican Republic. While we never talked about our feelings and how we were experiencing the world, my mom kept us busy in hopes we would persevere and be successful in life. In a family that experienced poverty, we were abundant in all other areas and I wanted to share that abundance with others.

NOT AN EASY ROAD

When I went to college as an Educational Opportunity Program (EOP) participant, I knew that I wanted a career that would allow me the opportunity to support people in achieving their goals. Being the youngest of five and seeing four siblings go to college, it seemed the natural thing to do so I followed them to SUNY Albany. A few of my childhood friends accompanied me as well.

Outside of the students in the EOP program and my friends, the campus was mostly white. I had never seen so many white folks in my life! In the classroom I felt invisible. I felt insignificant. I was always one of a few students of color in most of my classes. I was afraid that I was not smart enough and that I would fail. I chose psychology as a major because I wanted to understand why my life was the way it was. I joined the Latinx organization on campus, La Fuerza Latina as well as the Black student organization, ASUBA in hopes of connecting with my newly found Afro-Latinx identity. I was also seeking connections outside of my family and friends on campus.

In search of a new identity and new experiences, I eventually transferred to SUNY Stony Brook, where I did not know anyone. There were few students of color on campus and I found it hard at first to make new friends. I felt lonely. I felt out of place. I felt inadequate. My EOP advisor suggested that leaving SUNY Albany would be the worst decision that I would ever make. I was scared and transferred anyway.

Eventually I met a really great friend who invited me to an information session for the social work major at SUNY Stony Brook and that is when I made the decision that social work was for me. I was intrigued by this career possibility that was about social justice and supporting people in their life's journey. I also appreciated the diversity in disciplines within social work and the variability of ways to create impact within the profession. When I got back to my room that day, I rearranged my classes for the following semester so that I would be eligible to apply to the social work major.

It was at Stony Brook's Social Welfare program that I learned the words and phrases that described the world that I had experienced up until that point as a Black Latinx, living in poverty, in New York City. In class we would discuss, "The Poor" and deep down inside, the shame and embarrassment engulfed me.

I learned about words like institutional racism and oppression for the very first time. Institutional racism, also known as systemic racism, is a form of racism that is entrenched in a society through policies, laws, rules and regulations within a society or within an organization. I learned about how racist policies lead to discrimination in education, housing, health care, employment and the criminal justice system.

I felt betrayed and cheated. Why did it take so long for me to learn about racism being an institutional issue, and ways to work towards disrupting systems of oppression and inequity? I finally had the words to describe the injustices that I saw in my community and around the world. There were facets of social work that were troubling to me, and I always knew that at some point I would want to be part of making shifts within social work.

I knew that I wanted to create impact, but was not sure how I would do it. I knew that I was tired of being on welfare and living in poverty. I decided that I wanted to begin my career working with children and families experiencing poverty. The majority of my classmates were White women, and my professors were also mostly White. Whenever there was discussion about communities of color, sometimes the faculty looked at me and my other classmates of color, as if we were to educate the class.

During my internship experiences, I observed social worker burnout, poor management decisions, and financial distress. I also felt that there was limited representation of Black Latinx in administrative roles, and I wanted to explore the possibility of my interest in this area.

After graduate school, I returned to the Bronx and worked in the field of adolescent mental health, child welfare, and then school social work. I was a school social worker in the Bronx for eight years, where I worked with school staff, administrators, children, and their families, providing counseling, capacity building, education, advocacy, and training support. It made a difference that I knew the culture, that I spoke the language, and that I had the leadership skills to navigate the systems and have conversations about inequities and injustice within the school systems.

My career trajectory provided me with the knowledge, skills, and exposure necessary to effectively execute my role. It was not always easy. There were days that I talked myself out of being scared to say something. There were many moments where I enacted my agency and had to address institutional racism and oppression within the systems that I worked in. There were uncomfortable moments where policies did not align with my values, and I had to make difficult decisions as a social worker regarding ethics and equity.

My opinion was not always popular—and I persevered anyway. I began to realize the importance of building community, both in and out of work spaces, so that I felt supported, nurtured, and re-invigorated in the work. In my career trajectory, no one discussed the challenges around leading as a person of color. No one shared the joys of being representative of your culture and heritage. No one shared the challenges of being disregarded, dismissed, discounted, and misunderstood. No one shared how exhausting it could be grappling with microaggressions and racism in the workplace.

I did not get training in my coursework around engaging in difficult conversations while maintaining your integrity and honor. Another important aspect of being able to lead with excellence was being able to take time to practice self-care. It was only after I was immersed in the social work profession and started to feel burn-out that I learned about self-care and its importance. Self-care is for everyone, especially for those of us in a field that could be draining physically and emotionally. In fact, recently, the NASW Code of Ethics was revised to include self-care. Finally! All my life, I was learning about self-care through rest, joy, and fun practice, and did not realize it.

Self-care are activities that you do regularly to pour into your mind, body, and spirit. Taking time to self-reflect, rest, experience joy, and fun are all aspects of self-care. The practice of self-care supported my ability to bounce back when there were obstacles and challenges along my life's path, such as losing my dad on the Flight 587 plane crash in 2001.

TRAGEDIES AND TRIUMPHS

I became a divorcee and a single mother, while working multiple jobs. Being a single mother was very stressful and I am grateful to have had the support of my family and friends. I began researching doctoral programs. With the help of my village, I was able to take a leap and leave my school social work job and take on an associate director position at Columbia School of Social Work. I was scared and applied anyway.

I began taking non-matriculated doctoral courses and my confidence in who I was and what I brought to the field strengthened. Here, I was enhancing my career trajectory and feeling grand, but could not help but feel like a failure because my marriage had failed. I sought counseling support, as I wanted to be fully present for myself and my children. I continued to build my supportive village. Eventually I remarried, and through the encouragement of my husband and colleagues in the field department, I applied to the CUNY Graduate Center's PhD program in Urban Education. I worked full-time, raised my children, and was my mother's caregiver.

It was while in my program that I began to enhance my spiritual practices and build more networks of powerful women healers to support my overall wellness. I also began to learn more about my ancestors and how to honor them in all that I was doing. I was able to tap into family traditions that included daily prayer, meditation, lighting candles, incense, using herbs such as *palo santos*, and sage to cleanse my surroundings of negative energy.

I also learned of essential oils and meditation practices that helped me get back to me. Connecting with my spirit guides and ancestors was something I grew up observing, although my family did not discuss it until I got older and began asking questions. As a self-care tool, I also began writing a young adult novel loosely based on my life, *Born to Live*, where I share a coming-of-age story layered with life lessons and powerful context into institutional racism and our relationship with the world. These practices continue sustaining me and helping me connect with my inner wisdom and intuition in a deeper, more meaningful way.

In 2017, I co-founded Velocity Visions, Inc. with a colleague to work with organizations on enhancing the wellbeing and productivity of their staff. By creating a brave space, Velocity Visions, Inc. engages participants in activities and experiential exercises that promotes self-awareness, sharing, self-reflection, and personal and professional evolution. We are currently offering professional development opportunities in the areas of social emotional learning, healing centered practice, diversity equity and inclusion, and in self-care and burnout prevention. Through our work, hundreds of people have experienced healing, transformation, and impact. During the global pandemic, we created a podcast, "Self-Care to Success in 15 minutes or less," to share self-care strategies with the world.

When COVID-19 struck the nation, I was able to work from home while caring for my aging mother with Alzheimer's and my children. In April of 2021, my mother died of COVID-19. I am grateful for the lessons of rest, joy, and fun that she and my dad instilled in me. During my grieving process, I have given myself permission to receive support and center my self-care. Doing that has given me the ability to dive deeper in my life's purpose.

Currently, I am a full-time doctoral lecturer at the Department of Social Work at the College of Staten Island, CUNY. I see my role as integral to moving our profession to where it needs to be, while growing with the new generation of social workers.

In spite of all of the challenges I have experienced, radical self-care has sustained me and has given me the inner wisdom to persevere. Many of my ancestors did not have the privilege to rest. However, their resilience also includes stories of joy and practices around wellness and creating fun despite the challenges. I invite you to do the same. I leave you with a few questions for you to ask yourself, whatever stage you are in your career trajectory. My invitation is that you ask these questions absent of judgement. Notice what comes up for you, and explore what adjustments may be needed for you to succeed in strengthening your radical self-care.

REFLECTION

Social work is a profession that is needed now more than ever. In particular, we are in need of more social workers that can speak to the unique individual needs of the Latinx community. Social workers work to strengthen, rebuild and often build bridges to enhance the lives of individuals, groups and communities.

Social workers have an opportunity to be nepantleras. Gloria Anzaldúa described nepantleras as, "...the supreme border crossers...They serve as agents of awakening, inspire and challenge others to deeper awareness, greater *conocimiento* [intuitive way of outwardly expressing social justice], serve as reminder of each other's search for wholeness of being (Anzaldúa et al., 2003, p. 19)."

It is time to center our communities' strengths. It's time to have courageous conversations about racism, inequities in our communities, and work together to reimagine a world where we prioritize everyone's humanity and gifts.

Anzaldúa, G.E., Ortiz, S.j., Hernández-Avila, I., & Perez, D. (2003). Speaking across the divide. *Studies in American Indian Literatures*, 15 (¾), 7-22.

- What are you doing to consistently practice self-care?
- Are you giving yourself permission to rest? Are you allowing time for fun?
- How often do you access joy in your life?

ABOUT THE AUTHOR

Dr. Cindy Bautista-Thomas is an innovative visionary committed to helping others tap into their hidden potential, discover their God given gifts, and help them take inspired action towards creating the life they've always envisioned. She is a first-generation Dominican American who was born and raised in the Bronx, NY. She is also a licensed clinical social worker, educator, podcast host, yoga and mindfulness instructor, author, mother, wife, master trainer and curator of spaces of healing.

In 2017, Cindy decided to leverage her leadership, interpersonal, and facilitation skills and co-founded Velocity Visions, a company whose mission is to provide healing, transformation and impact to individuals, groups, and corporations through wellness activities, workshops, and interactive exercises that enhance personal and professional efficacy. With her bigger than life personality, warm smile, and innate ability to help others feel comfortable, Cindy is using her God given talents to help others find theirs. Her strong presence, passion, and professionalism makes Cindy one of the premiere trainers in the industry.

When she's not transforming lives, Cindy spends her time with her family and pursuing her creative passion of writing. To learn more about Cindy and the work she does with Velocity Visions, Inc. visit their website at www.velocityvisionsinc.com.

ERICA PRISCILLA SANDOVAL, LCSW-SIFI

EXECUTIVE BIOGRAPHY

Erica Priscilla Sandoval, LCSW-SIFI is Founder of Sandoval CoLab, a psychotherapy and consulting group. As a passionate, licensed clinical therapist and consultant, she is dedicated to promoting diversity, equity, and inclusion (DEI). She is committed to amplifying the voices and businesses of incredible Latinx social work leaders and social justice-focused changemakers, who are healing and inspiring communities.

She partners with organizations, universities, nonprofits, health care facilities, medical, and corporate professionals to provide access to resources to advance teams and help employees and students thrive. Most recently, she co-founded Employee Network Allyance, a space for allyship for today and tomorrow's employee network leaders who help each other succeed.

Erica holds a post master's degree in clinical adolescent psychology and a master's in social work from New York University, Silver School of Social Work. She currently serves as a volunteer leader as president of the board of directors for National Association of Social Workers NYC, the largest organization for professional social workers worldwide.

Her work focuses on the intersectionality of behavioral health, social disparities, trauma, and human development. She serves as advisor for Latino Social Work Coalition and Prospanica NY. Her successful career earned her numerous awards. She is regularly invited to be a guest speaker, moderator, and panelist by well-known organizations. Her greatest pride is raising her twenty-one-year-old daughter, Isabella, as a single mother, who she considers her biggest teacher. As a proud immigrant from Ecuador, her passion is fueled by supporting the community she is a part of.

Erica Priscilla Sandoval, LCSW-SIFI,
President and Founder of Latinx in Social Work Inc.
Erica@latinxinsocialwork.com
http://www.latinxinsocialwork.com/
https://www.sandovalcolab.com/

Made in the USA
Middletown, DE
16 October 2021

50367171R00156